# Fatherless Behavior

By

R. Poppy Lampkin, PhD

Fatherless Behavior

Copyright © 2022 by Robert Poppy Lampkin

All rights reserved. No part of this book may be used or reproduced without the publisher's permission, except with brief quotations in articles and reviews. For more information, visit www.serenityobtained.life.

ISBN: 978-0-9845611-7-9

Published by Serenity Obtained Media

The author may have changed the names, details, and circumstances to protect the privacy of those mentioned in this publication. The author did not edit or change any letters in "Letters to My Fathers" to maintain authenticity.

This publication does not substitute the advice of health care professionals.

# Table of Contents

GRATITUDE ..................................................................1

INTRODUCTION .........................................................6

## ONE
WHAT IS GRIEF? ......................................................10

## TWO
WHAT IS A FATHER? ...............................................15

## THREE
DADDY'S GIRL ..........................................................24

## FOUR
FATHERLESS BOYS ..................................................33

## FIVE
CHANGING THE NARRATIVE .................................40

## SIX
THERE ARE NO EXCUSES ......................................56

# SEVEN
MAKING AMENDS ...................................................................66

# EIGHT
PARENTAL ALIENATION ........................................................72

# NINE
ON THEIR BEHALF .................................................................82

# TEN
ONE LAST THING ...................................................................86

# ELEVEN
LETTERS TO MY FATHER.......................................................89

# GRATITUDE

Before completing this book, Rev. Tracey Flemmons, with the City of Houston, invited me to speak to a youth group about grief and loss. I kept coming up with the same cookie counter presentation I had done countless times to prepare for the presentation.

Since I wasn't aware of the age group of my audience, I decided I would engage them by simply asking what loss and grief meant to them rather than just talking about those issues in the context of death.

After assuring them that there were no wrong answers and no judgment, they defined loss and grief, sharing unsolicited examples of their own lives. The floodgates opened deep and wide when I validated their thoughts and answers.

Some of these beautiful children spoke openly about their losses, their pain, and their journey of navigating their grief. Boldly, they told their truth and showed empathy toward one another. Some of their parents were in the room, and I could see them quietly weeping and shaking their heads.

It was a powerful and spiritual experience that reshaped my understanding of loss and grief with young people. One mother whose grandchild took part in the group shared with me she never equated her granddaughter's behavior with her father's absence.

As I drove home with the radio off, I reflected on their voices, hurt, and pain. I replayed my interactions with them, and my heart exploded with joy that they could identify their feelings and were on the road to healing. They did not know how they spoke to my soul and my heart.

The youth of the New Day Deliverance Holiness Church, under the leadership of Apostle Taylor and First Lady Taylor, spoke to me so strongly that I came home and immediately began changing the manuscript of the book you're holding.

Thank you, Tracey Flemons, for the life-changing invitation. To you, the New Day Deliverance Holiness Church youth, thank you for your immense courage, transparency, and willingness to share your heart with me. Your contribution to this book is immeasurable.

I would not be the man I am today if it wasn't for my mother, Helen, and Ruby, my oldest sister. They would not allow me to fail in becoming an honorable man and a good human. They did this by any means necessary.

I caught my last whipping at 16 and in the presence of "my boys" because I disrespected my mother. One of my sisters came to the door and told me our mother wanted me to come in and finish my chores. Because I was with my boys, I shouted, "Tell her it can wait until I come in." The next person at the door was my mother, who calmly called me by first and middle name. I told my boys I would be right back.

As soon as I walked into the house, my mother pushed me with such force that I lost my balance and fell onto the sofa, which happened to be in front of a large window. She straddled me and proceeded to beat the living crap out of me. Even worse than the beating was the fact my boys were on the porch watching, laughing, and encouraging my mother to "get him." I think the humiliation hurt more than the whipping.

My sister, Ruby, taught me many things, but most importantly, to seek God and respect women. She did this by telling me what a man should and should not do regarding the treatment of a woman. When I was nine years old, we were sitting in the living room eating Blue Bell ice cream when someone asked me what I wanted to be when I grew up.

With pride, confidence, and my chest, I said I wanted to be a pimp. I had two uncles who were pimps, and all I knew was they had many beautiful girlfriends who loved them, wore the most amazing clothes, always had plenty of money, and drove a new car every year.

Who would not want those things? I was clueless as to the full scope of their "work." After a moment of silence, Ruby, Patsy, Jeannie, and Ruby Dell beat the brakes out of me for saying my career choice. I never spoke those words again.

Ruby held me accountable for my actions when I acted shady or thought I was a "playa." She also understood that our father could not teach me the morality of being an honorable man and gentleman and stood in the gap for me.

Thank you to all the mothers, sisters, aunts, and grandmothers who have stood by and those who have filled the void for their boys. It's not easy raising a boy, but without you, they would be lost.

# Serenity Obtained

# INTRODUCTION

While waiting to meet with a patient, I passed the time by scrolling Instagram. I am addicted to seeing babies who refuse to say "mama" and those who dance and sing, not to mention those who act like they're milk-drunk and 45 years old.

Today, instead of seeing reels and posts of babies and things that made me laugh, I saw something completely different. After seeing the first few posts on my timeline, I wondered if someone had hacked my account and questioned the changes to my usual algorithm.

Back-to-back was the most ratchet, World Star-esque, and ghetto-fabulous posts and reels I had ever seen. I watched girls doing things and dancing in such a sexual manner it would shame a stripper. Some reels embarrassed me.

I was shocked by a nineteen-year-old woman's revelation that her body count was between 50 and 60 sexual partners. Just when I thought I had heard everything, I saw an interview with a 16-year-old girl confessing that she has had four abortions because she doesn't want children at this time in her life. How messed up is that?

The violence with the boys was extreme and inhumane. I have witnessed much on social media and in life, but couldn't watch some reels my algorithm presented me.

The comments also caught my attention. Many of the comments were insensitive and judgmental. Comments such as chicken head, ratchet, hood-rat, THOT, Bop, ghetto-fabulous, 304s, to name a few.

However, two words caught my attention: "Fatherless Behavior." Those two words resonated with me throughout the day. Whenever I saw a post about a young person whose behavior was derogatory or ratchet, the words "Fatherless Behavior" came to mind.

**So, what is Fatherless Behavior?**

Google and the Urban Dictionary define fatherless behavior and daddy issues as psychological issues resulting from an absent, abusive, or problematic relationship with a father or father figure.

Social media would have us believe it is only about clicks or clout. I think clicks and clout are a minute part of it. I believe the underlying factor is grief.

Before we go any further, I need you to know that I don't believe all young people who do goofy or ratchet stuff on social media are fatherless or broken. As a therapist, I worked with young people with active parents in the home and have heard and seen all kinds of behaviors. I had both parents in my house, and trust me, I did many things I should not have done and things that could be fatherless behavior.

According to the U.S. Census Bureau, in 2020, 1 in 4 children lived without a biological, step, or adoptive father. That is 18.3 million children living in a single-parent home.

If you are one of the 18.3 million boys or girls ages 12-18, and your father is absent physically or emotionally. If you're angry, depressed, or simply not in a good space, this book may give insight into understanding why you do the things you do or feel the way you do. Grieving can be challenging no matter how old you are and where the grief stems from.

Whether you're Agnostic, Christian, Muslim, Mormon, Atheist, Hindu, Buddhist, or Wiccan, if you're navigating loss and grief, this book is for you. This book does not intend to shame or judge you. Its goal is to help you understand what may drive you from your purpose. I want you to understand YOUR why and find the path to a new and joyful you.

If you're an absent father, this book is for you. The book intends to show you the effects of your absence on your child's life and the pain and damage it inflicts. The book is also a guide to empower you to change the narrative between you and your child.

# *grief*

**Unique to each person.**

Every grief process is as different as each person grieving. Have grace with yourself as you learn what works best for you.

# ONE

## WHAT IS GRIEF?

Grief is a strong, sometimes overwhelming, emotion that we experience when we lose something like a parent, friend, job, boyfriend, girlfriend, or pet. You can grieve any loss that challenges your sense of normalcy or identity. Grief is a part of the fabric of life.

Some teens have lost more than one important person, and multiple losses can feel even more overwhelming. There are six basic principles of teen grief. These principles apply whether the grief results from death or an absentee father.

**Six basic principles of teen grief:**

1. Grieving is a teenager's natural reaction to death. Grief is a normal response to death and other losses. Losses such as an absent father, or a break-up from your boyfriend or girlfriend. It can even be from a best friend moving away. However, grieving does not feel natural because it may be difficult to control the emotions, thoughts, or physical feelings associated with death.

The sense of being out of control that is often a part of grief may overwhelm or frighten some teens. Grieving is normal, yet it may be an experience teens reject. Helping teens accept the reality that they are grievers allows them to do their grief work and to progress in their grief journey.

2. Each teen's grieving experience is unique. Grieving is a unique experience for each person. Teens grieve for different lengths of time and express various emotions. Grief is best understood as a process in which bodily sensations, feelings, thoughts, and behaviors surface in response to the death, its circumstances, the past relationship with the deceased, and the realization of the future without the person.

For example, sadness and crying may express grief for one teen, while another may respond with humor and laughter. Another may react with anger and unthinkable behaviors. The path of grieving is individual and often lonely. No book or grief therapist can predict or prescribe precisely what a teen will or should go through on their grief journey.

3. There is no right or wrong way to grieve. Sometimes, adults express strong opinions about "right" or "wrong" ways to grieve. But there is no correct way to grieve. The grieving process is individual and depends on many factors, including your personality, life experiences, faith, and the significance of the loss.

One cannot follow a simple pattern or set of rules when coping with death, nor can one evaluate this process. However, "helpful" and "unhelpful" choices and behaviors are associated with the grieving process. Some constructive behaviors encourage facing grief, such as talking with trusted friends, journaling, creating art, and expressing emotions rather than holding them inside.

Other grief responses are destructive and may cause long-term complications and consequences. For example, some teens attempt to escape their pain through many of the same escape routes adults choose. For some adults, it's alcohol and substance abuse, reckless sexual activity, antisocial behaviors, withdrawal from social activities, excessive sleeping, high risk-taking behaviors, and other methods that temporarily numb the pain of their loss. Young people are no different.

4. Each death is a unique experience. The way teenagers grieve differs according to personality and the particular relationship they have with the deceased.

They typically react in different ways to the death of a parent, sibling, grandparent, child, or friend. For many teens, peer relationships are primary. The death or loss of a boyfriend or girlfriend may seem to affect them more than the death of a sibling or grandparent.

5. Each person may mourn differently at different times within a family. One may be talkative, another may cry often, and a third might withdraw. This can generate great tension and misunderstanding within the already stressed family. Each person's response to death should be honored as their way of coping in that moment. Remember that responses may change daily or even from hour to hour.

6. Many issues influence the grieving process. The impact of a death on a teen relates to a combination of factors, including:

> ➢ Social support systems available for the teen (family, friends, and community)

- Circumstances of the death - how, where, and when the person died.
- Whether the young person discovered the body.
- Factors affecting the relationship with the deceased include: harmony, abuse, conflict, incompletion, and communication.
- The teen's level of involvement in the dying process, their emotional and developmental age of the teen, and their previous experience with death.

7. Grief is ongoing. It never ends, but it changes in character and intensity. Many grievers have compared their grieving to the constantly shifting tides of the ocean, ranging from calm, low tides to raging high tides that change with the seasons and the years. *Tyler Perry says, "Grief is a very living thing. It visits at random; you can't schedule it away, work it away, eat, drink, or sex it away–it will wait for you to finish."*

8. What does healing look like? To heal, acknowledge the pain. Trying to avoid feelings of sadness and loss only prolongs the grieving process. Healing from grief can mean feeling good about feeling good, making time for fun, and celebrating wonderful memories. It can also mean accepting life without the person who abandoned you or who passed away and creating fresh memories in the future.

Any man can be a father, but it takes someone special to be a dad

# TWO

## WHAT IS A FATHER?

**7 Essential Roles of a Dedicated Father**

Before we talk about grieving the loss of a father, let us define what a father is and what a father looks like. Anyone can father a child, but being a dad takes a lifetime. Fathers play a crucial role in every child's life that others cannot fill. This role can significantly impact children and help shape them into the people they become.

Fatherhood is a profound and transformative experience that goes beyond biological ties. Dads play a pivotal role in the family, shaping their children's lives and impacting their development. A father's guidance and presence are irreplaceable, creating a solid foundation for their children to thrive. We will explore the seven key roles that fathers embody, highlighting the significance of their contributions and responsibilities.

## **The Protector**

A father's role as protector is deeply ingrained in his being. He serves as a steadfast shield, diligently guarding his loved ones from harm and adversity, both physical and emotional. Fathers possess an innate instinct to prioritize the safety and well-being of their family, ensuring that their children feel secure and protected.

Whether it's teaching their kids to look both ways before crossing the street or comforting them during times of fear or distress, fathers stand tall as the guardians of their family's peace and security. Their unwavering presence and watchful eye provide stability and reassurance.

## **The Provider**

A father's unwavering dedication to meeting the family's financial needs is a testament to his commitment, steadfast love, and determination to provide a stable and nurturing environment.

They work tirelessly, often making selfless sacrifices and putting their desires and aspirations on hold to ensure their loved ones have a comfortable and secure life. From working long hours to pursuing additional opportunities for advancement, fathers go above and beyond to create a solid foundation upon which their families can thrive.

## **The Teacher**

Fathers are natural teachers, bestowing upon their children invaluable life lessons that will serve them for a lifetime. Through their guidance, dads instill crucial values, such as resilience, discipline, and integrity.

They serve as role models, shaping their children's character and equipping them with the essential tools to navigate life's inevitable challenges. From teaching them to tie their shoelaces to imparting wisdom about the importance of honesty and kindness, fathers play an integral role in shaping their children's moral compass. Their actions, as they lead by example, inspire their children to be the best versions of themselves.

## Mentor

A father's role as a mentor extends far beyond merely teaching life lessons. Dads inspire their children, nurturing their dreams and aspirations. They always guide and support their children, encouraging them to follow their dreams.

A father's belief in his child's potential can ignite an inner fire within them, propelling them towards remarkable achievements and personal growth.

## The Friend

While mothers often embrace the nurturing role, dads bring a unique friendship dynamic into the family. Dads engage in playful roughhousing, share infectious laughter, and create lasting memories. They become the rock upon which their children can always lean, offering a listening ear, words of wisdom, and a comforting presence that fosters a deep sense of trust and friendship.
.

## The Emotional Anchor

Fathers play a vital role in providing emotional stability and support within the family unit. They serve as the rock-solid shoulder to lean on during challenging times, offering reassurance, comfort, and a sense of security.

Dads teach their children the importance of emotional intelligence, encouraging them to express their feelings and navigate complex emotions in a healthy and constructive manner. Whether consoling a broken heart or offering guidance during hard decisions, then the father's role in the family cannot be explained in words.

## The Celebrant

Fathers wholeheartedly celebrate their children's achievements. Whether enthusiastically cheering at sports events or applauding academic accomplishments, dads take immense pride in their children's successes.

Their unwavering support and enthusiasm nurture their children's self-confidence, self-worth, and sense of achievement.

# THREE

## DADDY'S GIRL

When most people think of fatherlessness, they consider only two forms: death or divorce. Unfortunately, there are many forms of fatherlessness, and each one comes with its own trauma and reaction.

The forms of fatherlessness are Abandonment, Divorce, Death, Neglect, and Incarceration. What each has in common for most children is grief, which can lead to many issues and well into adulthood.

Many teenage girls and young women around the world suffer from emotional trauma because of father loss, whether it's caused by death, abandonment, divorce, imprisonment, addiction, or emotional or physical absence.

The father-daughter bond serves a separate but equally important purpose. Therapist Gary Brown, Ph.D., explains, "It would be difficult to overstate the powerful influence that fathers have in the shaping of their daughters' views about their self-image, values, sexuality, relationships, and the right to determine the course of their own lives."

A father holds the keys to his daughter's feminine identity, sense of self-worth, and future relationships. A dad's affirmation, or the lack thereof, will play a role in every aspect of her life, even influencing her choice of a marital partner.

There is a place in the female soul reserved for a dad or a daddy figure that will always yearn for affirmation. Not every girl is the same, of course, but almost every girl desires a close bond with the most significant man in her life.

She'll adore him if he loves and protects her and she feels safe in his arms. She will feel that way throughout life unless he disappoints her or until one of them dies. That relationship will: Shape how she views all men. If he rejects and ignores her, or worse, if he abuses and abandons her, the yearning within her becomes more intense, though it is often tainted with resentment and anger.

Let me clarify: although some of you will not like what I am about to write, mothers cannot fill this space. They can and must meet similar needs for love and adoration; in fact, they occupy their real estate in a daughter's heart.

A girl without a mother's love is a sad spectacle indeed, and I would not minimize the maternal role in any regard. But moms can't be dads, and dads can't be moms.

Let me elaborate on a fundamental question: why do girls and women have such intense needs for affirmation from their fathers, and why does the hurt caused by abandonment or rejection often reverberate for a lifetime?

As you'll recall, a primary reason for this inner ache is because a daughter's sense of self-worth and confidence is linked directly to her relationship with her dad. What he thinks about her and how he expresses his affection is a central source of her perceived value as a human being. It also affects her femininity and teaches her how to relate to boys and men.

Given this vital role in the development of girls, it is a tragedy that 34 percent of these precious babies are born into homes without a father present. The absence of a father deprives them of support and influence from birth!

Counselor and author H. Norman Wright addresses a woman's sense of identity in his outstanding book Always Daddy's Girl. It contains the following cogent observation addressed to the female reader:

Your relationship with your father was your critical initial interaction with the masculine gender. He was the first man whose attention you wanted to gain. He was the first man you flirted with, the first man to cuddle you and kiss you, the first man to prize you as a very special girl among all the other girls.

These experiences with your father were vital to the nurturing of the element that makes you different from him and all other men: your femininity. The fawning attention of a father for his daughter prepares her for her uniquely feminine role as a girlfriend, fiancée, and wife.

If something was lacking in your relationship with your father when you were a child, the development of your femininity suffered the most.

Why? As a little girl, you, by nature, expressed all the budding traits of the feminine gender. If your father was emotionally or physically absent or was harsh, rejecting, or angry toward you, you automatically and subconsciously attached his disapproval to your femininity.

You didn't have the intellectual capacity to understand his rejection, nor did you have the inner defensive structure to insulate yourself against it. You simply and naively reasoned, "I want Daddy to like me; Daddy doesn't like me the way I am; I will change the way I am, so Daddy will like me."

If a father does not value or respond to his daughter's femininity, it stunts her development. When a daughter has little experience in delighting her father as a child, she is incomplete. She must discover her femininity alone, often with tragic results in her relationships with men.

Wright's insightful analysis explains why some young women are so emotional about the rejection they feel from their fathers. It tells us why the most casual negative remark made by a dad years ago still echoes in his daughter's heart. It should also say something profound to today's fathers about their vulnerable little girls.

Research says he's right. Studies say active fathers contribute to higher self-esteem in young girls, lower rates of depression and anxiety, and a lower likelihood of childhood poverty. Research also suggests that affectionate fathers affect a child's cognitive and social development, offering them a prolonged state of security and protection, both physical and emotional.

Nothing replicates father-daughter affection's unique and irreplaceable quality outside the parent-child relationship. This uniqueness explains why the father-daughter bond is also the most fragile; it builds or breaks them.

Young girls need to experience unconditional love, especially in a world where they're constantly conditioned to believe that love comes with a cost, that love is supposed to hurt, and that to love someone is to labor for them. Girls need to know a love that doesn't have a limit on it and experience a love that isn't earned.

When a young girl does not experience unconditional love over the years, they become vulnerable young women who find it harder to build healthy personal and professional lives as they are building their lives, relationships, aspirations, and self-representation based on this trauma, mainly when it occurs during adolescence. They suffer from trust issues, low self-esteem, and fear of abandonment, which create the unhealthy need to be accepted and loved at all costs.

These symptoms often go unnoticed and unacknowledged, as these young women do not understand the root issue causing their behavior and build a façade around themselves.

Over the years, the fatherless daughter syndrome can present in several ways, ranging from dysfunctional behaviors and unhealthy relationships to chronic depression; it may even fade from awareness temporarily.

Instead, it gives rise to a vicious cycle of self-destruction mechanisms, self-doubt, and unhealthy or abusive relationships in their lives. Because when some girls feel unloved and unworthy, they often search for love and validation in all the wrong places, which makes them vulnerable to both physical and emotional abuse.

The social and economic environment, as well as the family structure, are factors that influence or reinforce the impact of fatherlessness on girls' and young women's lives.

In some low-income families where the father is absent, the mother is emotionally unavailable or unstable, and there is no positive male figure, daughters will most likely experience more self-worth issues, insecurities, abuse, sexual promiscuity, and repeat the cycle of fatherlessness.

Having a support system is of great importance in this context, as girls often feel vulnerable and struggle to open up about what they experience.

The numbers don't lie. Statistics show young people thrive with both healthy parents' active and meaningful relationships. Understanding the impact of the absent father in young women's lives, specifically the emotional trauma caused by father loss and the consequences on society, is critical to having a healthier society.

The emotional trauma caused by the father's loss not only weakens the girl but creates a void she will somehow try to fill by all means possible. Consequently, she becomes exposed to all forms of danger and abuse.

Fatherless young women often become self-destructive, violent, vulnerable, sexually promiscuous, prone to abuse, unstable, and develop a conflictual relationship with their femininity and sexuality. Social media bears this truth 24/7.

They find it difficult to trust and live in constant fear of abandonment, which sometimes leads them to make unhealthy choices for themselves to please others and feel accepted. Consistent feelings of rejection can cause teens to avoid being rejected or abandoned by others.

Avoiding abandonment at all costs becomes necessary for survival. If the possibility of abandonment is present, a teen might make suicide attempts or engage in self-harming behavior such as cutting, high-risk sexual behavior, or manipulative behavior.

Young women feel the impact of fathers' loss most strongly in their romantic relationships. Growing up, a father figure is like that of "The Perfect Man," a sort of a masculine ideal in a girl's mind. It's her first male reference, one that embodies the values necessary for her to build her identity: guidance, protection, authority, discipline, kindness, confidence, and absolute love.

When a young woman becomes an adult, this ideal (and illusory) image of her father and their relationship, or the relationship she longed for, heavily influences her choice of partners, resulting in unhealthy and often abusive relationships.

Many of these women will particularly struggle during separation and break-ups as they make an emotional projection of their dads on their partner. In contrast, others experience more difficulty trusting, expressing their feelings, and committing.

We expect that fatherless young women will unconsciously repeat relationship patterns marked by constant fear of abandonment, insecurity, difficulty opening up, conflict with male authority figures, and the use of defense mechanisms. They usually create a strong shell around themselves, but deep inside, they remain incredibly vulnerable.

Mothers play a fundamental role in building a positive identity and self-esteem in young women and girls. Still, most of the time, they lack the tools to understand their daughter's critical needs triggered by their father's absence.

And since they are unaware of it, they cannot rectify the issue. Sometimes, the presence of a stepfather or a strong male figure can be positive in the lives of fatherless young women; without filling the void or healing her wounds, it can provide the guidance, trust, and safety they need.

By recognizing the impact of Fatherless Daughter Syndrome and seeking therapeutic interventions and support networks, these daughters can embark on a journey of healing and empowerment.

Through counseling, self-reflection, and surrounding themselves with positive influences, they can learn to establish their self-worth, build healthy relationships, and break the cycle of fatherlessness.

Remember, you are not alone. Others have walked a similar path and understand the challenges you face. Reach out to support groups, seek professional help, and surround yourself with a community that uplifts and supports you.

# FOUR

## FATHERLESS BOYS

While working on this chapter, I watched a reel on Instagram in which four teens carjacked a 73-year-old woman. They drug this lady to the point her arm was severed from her body. They did this in broad, open daylight and as other cars passed. She died because of her injuries. This was only one of many postings on social media of our boys showing how out of control they are.

An army of twelve million boys is roaming the nation without their biological fathers. Not all the boys are up to mischief or breaking the law. Some have no fathers because of death or misfortune. However, most are the products of irregular unions, broken families, and abandonment. Thus, the overwhelming majority are in conditions that are asking for trouble.

Fatherless boys represent a huge risk category. Numbering 12 million, they make up nearly a third of boys. These boys are more likely than those with biological fathers to join the ranks of those who commit crimes, drop out of school, and commit suicide. They are also much more likely to enter these paths than girls.

Most young men who commit mass shootings come from this troubled demographic.

One of the most critical social issues that affects children, especially sons, is the absence of dads. There are several causes for fathers not being there, including their own decision, their demise, or their incarceration.

But the ramifications of having a father who isn't there are profound and long-lasting, especially for sons. The effect that absent fathers have on abandoned sons and the effects that this relationship has on their development will be covered in this chapter.

Sons suffer when their fathers are absent. Sons who lack a father figure miss out on the direction, support, and nurturing only a father can offer. When their fathers are absent, sons may feel abandoned or rejected, since they frequently depend on them for emotional support, acceptance, and stability.

Boys who don't have a father in their lives consequently often have emotional imbalances, including wrath, fear, insecurities, or grief. They have trouble building relationships with new individuals and trusting them, which causes issues with attachment and mistrust.

Second, boys without father figures frequently lack male role models who can offer moral instruction on what it means to be a man and how to respect others.

When not present, youngsters could pick up lessons from their misguided peers or social media, which might not be the best role models.

The inability to set boundaries brought on by an absent father can subsequently harm relationships. Sons, for instance, may struggle to control their aggression and repress their emotions, which might cause subpar judgment and unhealthy coping techniques.

Third, boys of absent fathers are more likely to exhibit detrimental patterns of conduct and to be influenced by harmful social norms. Without the discipline and supervision that a father offers, this male may be more susceptible to negative peer influences, such as gang involvement, drug usage, or criminal activities.

Sons may experience difficulties in their romantic and family relationships. Insecurities brought on by this lack of a solid foundation in their lives may later develop into relationship issues.

What happens when a boy's father is absent and doesn't get taught the "lessons" he should have gotten from a loving father? Fathers are supposed to teach their sons many things about being a man. One of those lessons is how to be a man in love. Another is how to treat a woman when you're in love.

These fathering lessons help a son learn how to be a loving man. If you don't get the lessons because your father is absent, you must deal with the loss and look for it elsewhere. By the way, plenty of mothers have the maturity and wisdom to guide their sons into a stable adulthood. They wear two hats, so to speak, well.

Problems occur when sons seek fathering lessons in the wrong places and from the wrong people. If losing a father is not adequately grieved, it can turn to aggression and violence with the guidance of other men with unresolved loss turned to aggression and violence.

A son needs his father as a stable presence during his growth and development. Simply put, a son must feel that his daddy loves him. This simple emotion has a significant impact on how you perceive yourself and others. Giving and receiving love is easier when you don't feel compromised, especially if you feel loved. When your father loves you, you believe that being loved has something to do with having love to give.

If this simple need does not get met because of your father's absence, two things will happen: grief and a search for it somewhere else. The grief part is trying to deal with the loss.

If you are lucky enough to work through this feeling without too much self-criticism and self-blame (children like to blame themselves for things like an absent parent.), you'll naturally get to a point where you'll try to find the love you didn't get from your father somewhere else.

You have options. You can get it from your mother, other men in your family, coaches, teachers, or even male friends. The point is that you require love from your father and are trying to meet that need in other relationships.

Finally, because boys lack a male role model to serve as an example of what it is to be a man, sons of absent fathers may find it challenging to identify with their masculinity. Feelings of emasculation may result from this circumstance, which may further undermine one's confidence and self-worth.

Since dads are symbols of stability and authority, their absence may impact how sons regard themselves and their value in society, resulting in a lack of self-confidence.

To heal from an absent father, you can acknowledge and process your emotions, cultivate self-compassion, seek professional support if needed, learn to forgive, set healthy boundaries, and build positive relationships with other supportive figures in your life; allowing yourself to grieve the loss of a father figure is also crucial to the healing process.

**Key steps to consider:**
Acknowledge your feelings.
Don't suppress your emotions; allow yourself to feel anger, sadness, disappointment, or confusion related to your father's absence.

**Practice self-compassion**
Be kind to yourself and understand that you are not to blame for your father's actions.

**Seek professional help**
Therapy can provide a safe space to explore your feelings, understand the impact of your father's absence, and develop coping mechanisms.

**Journaling**
Writing your thoughts and feelings about your father can help you process them and gain clarity.

**Build a support system**
Lean on trusted friends, family members, or mentors who can offer emotional support and understanding.

**Learn to forgive**
While forgiveness may not mean reconciliation with your father, it can help you release resentment and move forward.

**Set boundaries**

If your father attempts to re-enter your life, establish clear boundaries based on what is healthy for you.

**Focus on self-esteem**

Work on building a positive self-image and recognizing your worth independent of your father's presence.

Any man can be a father, but it takes someone special to be a dad

# FIVE

## CHANGING THE NARRATIVE

When I was a therapist working at a psychiatric treatment facility with adolescents who came from single-parent homes and, or severely dysfunctional families, I couldn't imagine some of them returning to that same environment and staying healthy.

However, I learned from some young people that the human spirit can be indomitable. I saw kids who not only survived but thrived and became successful adults with healthy families of their own.

If you want to change the narrative in your life, it is ABSOLUTELY possible with honesty, determination, and support.

If your father has abandoned you, you have suffered trauma. Childhood trauma, to be exact. Feeling neglected or abandoned can be traumatizing. Processing trauma takes time. Understanding what has happened in your life and, more importantly, that you did nothing to cause your father to leave or reject you is vital to your journey of healing.

There are things you can do to overcome the negative impact of growing up without a father. While the people in your life can impact your feelings, they don't determine your future.

You can choose the course of your life. Countless men and women of greatness tell you they feel your pain, but you must trust in the journey. You may face more complicated challenges than others with fathers.

However, you still get to write the story of your life. Here are some things you can do to overcome the emotional impact of absent fatherhood.

**Allow yourself to grieve.**

Growing up without a dad can be painful. You may believe you missed out on parts of your childhood. Many people associate grieving with the death of a loved one, but all different losses can lead to suffering — and an absent parent can be one of them.

You may find that to start your emotional healing process, you must allow yourself to grieve what you have lost. This loss could be the relationship with your father that you had in your life or the relationship that you never could have. You may grieve the father you lost or the fantasy father you always wanted.

Grieving may help you acknowledge the loss that your father has intentionally or unintentionally left in your life. It may be just what you need to help you work through the emotional impact that the absence caused.

**Focus on building your self-esteem.**

You may struggle with low self-esteem even if you don't actively consider it. Low self-esteem can lead individuals to become people-pleasers, constantly seeking the approval of others. If you rarely believe you are "good enough," it could be a sign that you're experiencing challenges with your self-esteem.

You can build your self-esteem by practicing self-compassion, spending time with people who accept you for who you are, and engaging in activities you love that make you feel good about yourself.

**Find a mentor you can count on.**

While you may never replace the exact relationship you could have had if your father was involved in your life, you may benefit from finding someone who can fill some of that role.

It's believed that having an active "father figure" can help prevent both behavioral and psychological problems.

This person, whether they are a trustworthy stepdad, grandfather, coach, teacher, counselor, or any other figure who takes on some fatherly role, can be a source of comfort and guidance. Having someone to talk to about things you would discuss with your dad if he were around or having a supportive adult to do activities with can be incredibly beneficial.

This individual can impart knowledge and offer words of wisdom that your dad may not have shared or that you wouldn't have received otherwise. Their guidance can be a source of enlightenment and empowerment for you.

Your relationship with your mother can also provide guidance and comfort. A mom can often give enough support and love to a child. Recognizing and seeking this support can empower you in your journey.

**Learn how to have healthy relationships.**

Your father's absence may cause you to struggle with other relationships. You may be afraid that you can't depend on others, or you may automatically expect the people who love you to eventually leave. Or you may subconsciously try to connect with others to make up for what you didn't receive from your dad.

Suppose you believe that you're having difficulties with your relationships. In that case, you may benefit from talking with a trusted older individual who can provide feedback and guidance. Many books can also offer beneficial life tips, including information on relationship development.

**Let go of the shame and guilt.**

In coping with the loss and grief of an absent father, you may have done things in your life that you are not proud of.

To mask your pain, you may have behaved in a way that caused emotional harm to another person.

- ❖ Gossip can be difficult to avoid as a teen. There is a sense of peer pressure to join in the hurtful communication.

- ❖ Bullying is similar in that there is peer pressure to join in. To defend the person who is being bullied is to invite judgment. We may fear that our friends may look at us differently and no longer want us around.

❖ Arguments happen, and they happen with those we love or are close to. In the heat of the moment, we sometimes say things we didn't mean and later regret.

When we behave in a way that does not align with our values, we may feel a sense of guilt. Guilt can be a motivating emotion that can be helpful. Sometimes, guilt can transition into shame and cause you significant harm. It is essential to understand the distinction between guilt and shame.

**Guilt and shame are similar, yet distinct.**

There are many similarities between guilt and shame. Neither emotion is fun to feel and experience and can cause sadness, regret, and disappointment. Yet, there are subtle differences between guilt and shame, and they affect a teen in dramatically different ways.

**What is guilt?**

Guilt is the overwhelming feeling you get when you do or feel you did something wrong. Many teens feel guilty because they think they're the reason their father is absent. We often feel guilty in private, a feeling elicited by our negative thoughts and self-appraisal.

**Guilt is an emotion that can affect teenagers, including:**

❖ Self-condemnation: Guilt can be a feeling of self-condemnation for doing something wrong or inappropriate.

❖ Self-appraisal: Negative thoughts and self-appraisal can elicit guilt.

❖ Interference with daily functioning: Guilt can interfere with a teen's ability to focus, concentrate, and sleep.

❖ Mental health concerns: Guilt can lead to depression, anxiety, and nightmares.

❖ Isolation: Guilt can lead to a teen isolating.

❖ Self-harm: Guilt can lead a teen to talk about harming themselves.

❖ Physical symptoms: Excessive guilt can cause physical symptoms such as muscle tension.

❖ Victimization: Adolescents with high levels of guilt may experience more physical, verbal, and relational victimization.

Guilt can have benefits, such as self-improvement, personal growth, and recognizing strengths and weaknesses. However, it can also negatively affect a teen's mental health. The most important thing for you to remember is that you are not responsible for your father's absence.

**What is Shame?**

We can view shame as a feeling of discomfort that accompanies the belief that one is unworthy of love and good things and is deeply flawed. Beliefs can fuel it about oneself and the world around one.

Shame is like a living, breathing creature that lives inside and attaches to a teen's soul. Like any other living creature, it needs food to survive. The food that shame feeds upon is secrecy.

Teens who feel shame are often embarrassed to talk about what they are experiencing. Your parents will attempt to get you to open up, as they sense something is wrong.

The longer you keep your thoughts and feelings about shame secret, the more the shame creature is fed. The more the shame creature is fed, the stronger it gets. A more powerful shame creature increasingly controls your self-perception.

**Teens will often start thinking and feeling:**

- ❖ "I'm just broken. No one will understand, and no one can help."

- ❖ "Maybe I'm just a bad person. I don't want to change, and my parents will never accept me for who I am."

- ❖ "I'm weak and worthless. If I were stronger, I could stop (insert behavior here)."

Shame perpetuates a vicious cycle: the worse you feel, the more ashamed you feel. The greater your shame, the more you repress your thoughts and feelings.

The more you stuff, the more you feed the shame creature, and the stronger it gets. Increasing intensity will bring more shame, thus continuing the cycle.

I will remind you again you are not responsible for your father's absence, and no matter what you did to fill the void, it is not a death sentence. Forgive yourself and change your narrative.

**Forgive your father**

This is probably the last thing you want to hear about the person who has caused you the most pain. I get it. And here is what I learned about forgiveness during my grief journey.

On my journey of forgiveness, I learned one should not blindly forgive someone. Before you forgive, allow yourself to feel the full force of the anger in yourself. Allow yourself to fully feel the anger that is present because once you do, it will dissipate; you will let go of it. Don't do it to forgive. Do it to free yourself so that forgiveness is not for the other person–it is for yourself.

Your dad may not even realize the hurt they have caused you. Alternatively, they may have been absent because of circumstances beyond their control. Worse yet, he may not even care about the pain his absence caused.

If you're carrying resentment and bitterness toward your father, it's likely hurting your emotional and mental health as well.

Choosing to forgive your dad doesn't mean that you excuse his behavior or lack of attention that you received; it simply means that you will not let your anger continue to have power over your life. You don't have to reconcile or have contact with your father, but choosing forgiveness can help you move forward more healthily.

**Your Purpose**

One evening, I was interviewing a young man for admission to an adolescent psychiatric unit. According to his parents, his behavior was out of control, and he had become self-destructive, using drugs and engaging in high-risk behaviors.

For the sake of anonymity, I will call him James. During the interview, James presented as a kind, soft-spoken young man who arrived at the unit high on acid, weed, and mushrooms. He was the picture of a hot mess.

While we talked, James drew a picture that I still have forty-plus years later. The picture was filled with vibrant colors, intricate details, and the names of drugs written within exotic mandalas. It was a complete work of art, and even more impressive, it was completed in less than an hour.

Long story short, through intensive therapy, James identified his issues and addressed his pain, anger, and shame. He discovered himself and his purpose. Needing more structure after leaving the facility, he joined the Air Force. He is now one of the world's most sought-after international cyberterrorism experts and owns his own company.

It does not happen overnight, but it is never too late to identify or change your path. But how do you find your purpose if it's not obvious to you? Is it something you develop naturally throughout a lifetime, or can you take steps to encourage more purpose in your life?

**Here are some recommendations;**

**1. Identify the things you care about**

Purpose is all about applying your skills toward contributing to the greater good in a way that matters to you. So identifying what you care about is an important first step.

**2. Reflect on what matters most**

Sometimes, it's hard to single out one or two things that matter most to you because your circle of care and concern is far-ranging. Understanding what you value most may help you narrow your life purpose to something manageable that also truly resonates with you.

**3. Recognize your strengths and talents**

We all have strengths and skills that we've developed over our lifetimes, which help make up our unique personalities. Yet some of us may be unsure of what we offer.

It's helpful to ask others—teachers, friends, family, colleagues, mentors—for input. Try sending emails to five people who know you well and pose questions like:

What do you think I'm good at?

What do you think I enjoy?

How do you think I'll leave my mark on the world?

**4. Try volunteering**

Finding purpose involves more than self-reflection. It's also about trying out new things and seeing how those activities enable you to use your skills to make a meaningful difference in the world.

Volunteering in a community organization focused on something of interest to you could provide you with some experience and do good at the same time.

Working with an organization serving others can connect you with people who share your passions and inspire you. With others' support, it's easier to find and sustain purpose. Volunteering has the added benefit of improving our health and longevity, at least for some people.

However, not all volunteer activities lead to a sense of purpose. "Sometimes volunteering can be deadening," says Stanford University researcher Anne Colby. It needs to be engaging. You need to feel you're achieving something. When you find a good match, volunteering will "feel right"—it won't be draining but invigorating.

**5. Imagine your best possible self**

Imagine yourself at 40 if everything had gone as well as it could have in their lives. Then, answer these questions:

What are you doing?

What is important to you?

What are you passionate about, and why?

The why is important because purposes usually emerge from our reasons for caring.

**6. Cultivate positive emotions like gratitude and awe**

To find purpose, it helps to foster positive emotions, such as awe and gratitude. That's because these emotions are tied to well-being, empathy toward others, and finding meaning in life, all of which help us focus on how we can contribute to the world.

Practicing gratitude helps point one toward purpose. Reflecting on the blessings of your life often leads us to "pay it forward," which is how gratitude can lead to purpose.

There are many ways to cultivate awe and gratitude. Awe can be inspired by seeing the beauty in nature or recalling an inspirational moment. Gratitude can be practiced by keeping a gratitude journal or writing a gratitude letter to someone who helped you in your life.

Whatever tools you use, developing gratitude and awe has the added benefit of being good for your emotional well-being, which can give you the energy and motivation you need to carry out your purposeful goals.

**7. Look at the people you admire**

Sometimes the people we admire most tell us how we might want to contribute to making a better world for ourselves. Reading about the work of civil rights leaders or climate activists can give us a moral uplift, motivating us to work toward the greater good. Do not trust social media!

However, sometimes looking at these larger-than-life examples can be too intimidating. Instead, you can look for everyday people doing good in smaller ways. Maybe you have a friend who volunteers to collect food for the homeless or a family friend whose work in promoting social justice inspires you.

You don't need fame to fulfill your purpose in life. You just need to look at your inner compass—and start taking small steps in the direction that means the most to you.

**Last but not least**

Growing up with a physically or emotionally absent father can lead to a range of emotional impacts, but how it affects one person won't apply to another. While specific traumatic experiences can have a lasting effect, it's also possible to overcome and move past your loss.

Remember this: Asking for help and support without judgment is alright. A therapist can help you process the past and look forward to the future. A therapist can guide you to understand your why and how to move forward.

They can also teach you skills that may improve the quality of your relationships as you move forward in life. It's often challenging to discuss trauma and loss, yet you can find therapists offering both in-person and online appointments. The bottom line is that a therapist can also help you begin the healing process.

**Self-Compassion**

In the previous chapter, we discussed the importance of forgiving the absent father. Now let's talk about you. First, I need you to know that there is good news for you no matter what negative, terrible, horrible, or unspeakable thing you have done in the past or even yesterday. NOTHING that enters your life is able or sufficient to separate you from God's love for you.

According to Dr. Kristin Neff, self-compassion does not differ from compassion for others. Think about what the experience of compassion feels like. First, you notice others are suffering, allowing you to develop compassion for them.

If you ignore that homeless person on the street, you can't feel sympathy for how difficult their experience is.

Second, compassion involves feeling moved by others' suffering so that your heart responds to their pain (the word compassion means to "suffer with"). When this occurs, you feel warmth, caring, and the desire to help the suffering person.

Compassion also means offering understanding and kindness to others when they fail or make mistakes, rather than harshly judging them. Finally, when you feel sympathy for another (rather than pity), you realize that suffering, failure, and imperfection are part of the shared human experience.

Self-compassion involves acting the same way toward yourself when you are having a difficult time, fail, or notice something you don't like about yourself. Instead of simply ignoring your pain with a "stiff upper lip" mentality, you stop to tell yourself, "This is hard right now. How can I comfort and care for myself at this moment?"

Self-compassion is about treating yourself with kindness and understanding for your failings, not criticizing yourself mercilessly—perfection is unrealistic.

Improving yourself is about caring for yourself, not fixing flaws. Most importantly, having compassion for yourself means you honor and accept your humanness.

Things will not always go the way you want them to. You will encounter frustrations, losses, mistakes, and bumps against your limitations and fall short of your ideals. This is the human condition, a reality shared by all of us.

The more you open your heart to this reality instead of constantly fighting against it, the more you will feel compassion for yourself and all your fellow humans in the experience of life.

# SIX

## THERE ARE NO EXCUSES

This chapter is not for the absent father who is absent because of a mother who is standing in the way of a father's relationship with his child.

This chapter is about men who don't pay child support and men who pay but choose not to be emotionally involved with their children. It is for the men who are the best stepfathers but an absent father to their biological children. This is also for the father who is incarcerated.

After reading this book, I hope you will feel the need to reach out to your child and begin making amends for your absence, regardless of your child's age. It's never too late.

Arah Iloabugichukwu, author of *Of Mothers & Daughters*, wrote a raw and profound article in Medium titled Black Fathers Weren't Removed from the Home; They Left.

In Arah's scathing article on fatherlessness, she states, "Black men weren't removed from their homes; they got up and left. They made the same choice in the 1950s, 1960s, 1970s, 1980s, 1990s, and 2000s that they continue to make today, a decision that says children are an extension of the women who carry them, and when that attachment is severed, the children are renounced right along with it.

Our great-grandmothers weren't lying about these men who, while married, carelessly sprinkled their seeds around the city and then left those seeds to fend for themselves. Our grandmothers were fighting to salvage their sickly reputations while these men did everything in their power to destroy the seeds under their surname.

There is no Black anti-father task force picking the world's best Black dads up from soccer practice, never to be seen again. The real conspiracy is they don't desire to be there."

I couldn't agree more with Ms. Iloabugichukwu's perspective on black fatherlessness. However, to prepare for this book, I spoke with a multiethnic group of 120 young men and women about fatherlessness and its impact on their lives. Some of their letters and quotes are in this chapter.

Therefore, I am forced to be more inclusive in my critique of absent fathers. Black men may be the largest demographic of absent fathers, but they are not the only ones. In 2023, 50% of Black children were living in homes without a father versus 20% of White children and 31% of Hispanic children. Asians had the lowest rate of 15%. 1% is too many. All children matter.

Systemic racism, white supremacy, paying child support, not paying child support, and incarceration, including the child's mother, should not be able to separate a father from an emotional connection to his child.

And yes, I am fully aware some women will keep the child from the father on the grounds the father no longer wants to be with the mother.

But I believe that the women who deliberately keep their children from their fathers are worse than the absent fathers. The next chapter speaks to these mothers.

One of my clients, who is a migrant, shared with me his story about what he endured to get his son medical help in America. He shared pictures of his travels through the Darien Gap. The Darien Gap is a dangerous jungle migrants travel through to reach the United States from South and Central America. The Darien Gap is a roadless, 60-mile stretch of dense rainforest, mountains, and swamps on the border of Colombia and Panama.

Migrants face many threats while crossing the Darien Gap. It is one of the rainiest and most dangerous places on the planet, a lawless, unpoliced region filled with drug smugglers, sex traffickers, and political rebels. The area is strewn with the skeletons of adults and children who perished there.

This migrant father left his wife and other children at home and walked this hell-on-earth parcel of land, carrying his terminally ill son on his back. He believed his child would receive excellent health care or, at worst, die with dignity in the United States.

Using an interpreter, he wept as he spoke about his fear of his journey and how important it was to him as a father to get his child onto American soil, even though he was breaking the law. He wanted his son to know that his father had done everything he could to give him a better life.

He is one of many fathers who walk across borders daily in search of a better life for their children, regardless of the odds against them, including a life that might not exist.

Yet we have fathers in America who have all the freedoms in the world but will not go the extra mile to assess the free federally funded resources and free legal representation that could get them into their child's life, that could save their child. Make it make sense.

According to author Iloabugichukwu, men using mobile devices frequently use social media to criticize the mothers of their children for perceived parenting obstacles.

**Your Daughter Needs You**

*"It took ten years, but I can finally utter a vast truth that caused me tremendous shame and sadness: My father didn't love me. I never spoke that deep, dark secret, but it always festered inside me. It manifested itself throughout my life as I struggled with a food obsession, low self-esteem, social anxiety, and depression."* Maria.

"Fathers provide their daughters with a masculine example. They teach their children about respect and boundaries and help put daughters at ease with other men throughout their lives. So, if she didn't grow up with a proper example, she would have less insight and be likelier to go for a man who would replicate her father's abandonment."

Below, you'll find six ways an uninvolved dad may affect a daughter.

## 1. Fatherless Daughters Have Self-Esteem Issues

According to Deborah Moskovitch, an author and divorce consultant, children often blame themselves when their dad leaves the home and becomes less involved in their lives. When they aren't explained why dad left, they make up their own scenario and wrongfully conclude that it's their fault and that they're unlovable.

This is especially true for daughters. Countless studies have shown that fatherlessness has a highly negative impact on daughters' self-esteem. If her father isn't there, her confidence in her abilities and value as a human can diminish. Academically, personally, professionally, physically, socially, and romantically, a woman's self-esteem is reduced in every setting if she does not form a healthy relationship with her father.

## 2. Daughters With Absent Fathers Struggle to Build and Maintain Relationships

According to Pamela Thomas, author of Fatherless Daughters (a book that examines how women cope with the loss of a father via death or divorce), women who grew up with absent dads find it difficult to form lasting relationships.

Because their dad's rejection scarred them, they didn't want to risk getting hurt again. Consciously or unconsciously, they avoid getting close to people. They may form superficial relationships in which they reveal little of themselves and put little effort into getting to know others. They may become promiscuous as a way of getting male attention without becoming too emotionally involved. Imagine a 16-year-old girl with 20 bodies.

**3. Women With Absent Fathers Are More Likely to Have Eating Disorders**

In their book, The Parent's Guide to Eating Disorders, authors Marcia Herrin and Nancy Matsumoto eloquently write about the fact that girls with physically or emotionally absent fathers are at greater risk of developing eating disorders.

Anorexia nervosa, bulimia, binge eating, body dysmorphia, unhealthy preoccupations with food or body weight, and other eating disorders are all more likely if a girl does not have a father figure as she's growing up.

Daughters without dads are also twice as likely to be obese. Because her longing for a close relationship with her dad is denied, she may develop what Margo Maine (author of Father Hunger: Fathers, Daughters, & Food) calls "father hunger," a deep emptiness and a profound insecurity. Daughters are left wondering: What's so wrong with me that my father doesn't love me? If I looked different, would I earn Daddy's love?

**4. Daughters of Absent Fathers Are More Prone to Depression**

Not surprisingly, girls who grew up with dads who were emotionally or physically absent are more likely to struggle with depression as adults. Because they fear abandonment and rejection, these women often isolate themselves emotionally.

They avoid healthy romantic relationships because they don't feel deserving and fear getting hurt, but they might jump into unhealthy relationships that ultimately lead to heartbreak.

In either scenario, the women are in emotional peril and frequently become depressed.

If they don't deal with the cause of their sadness and absence, they may never be able to develop healthy relationships with men. To top it all off, data suggests that children without fathers are more than twice as likely to commit suicide.

**5. Fatherless Daughters Are More Likely to Become Sexually Active Earlier**

Studies have shown the many benefits of a strong father-daughter bond. Most notably, girls who are close to their dads are less likely to get pregnant as teenagers. They delay engaging in sexual relationships and wait longer to get married and have children. When they find a husband, their marriages are more emotionally satisfying, stable, and long-lasting.

Countless studies also show that women who have unstable or absent paternal relationships are more likely to have sex earlier and engage in risky sexual behaviors. Daughters are four times more likely to get pregnant as a teen if dad isn't in the picture. Studies show that over 70% of unplanned teenage pregnancies occur in homes where there is no father.

**6. Abandoned Daughters Are Susceptible to Addiction**

As with depression, eating disorders, and low self-esteem, the absence of a father can trap a daughter in a negative, repetitive pattern she can't easily break out of and turn to drugs to self-medicate and help numb the pain.

She is more likely to find herself trapped in a cycle of substance abuse, for example. According to the U.S. Department of Health and Human Services, fatherless children are at a dramatically greater risk of drug and alcohol abuse.

Not only are kids in father-absent households about four times more likely to be poor (which can trigger many negative cycles), but fatherless adolescents were found to be 69% more likely to use drugs and 76% more likely to commit crimes.

## Your Son Needs You

An army of twelve million boys is roaming the nation without their biological fathers. Many are not in trouble but are at risk of a host of life-changing events. Those in trouble can still be saved and want to be saved. They want to take your hand and let you lead them.

One of the most significant psychological impacts of fatherlessness on sons is the development of low self-esteem. Fatherless boys often struggle with a sense of worthlessness and have difficulty forming positive self-concepts.

The absence of a father can lead to difficulties in social relationships, especially for boys who struggle to establish trust and intimacy with others. As a result, fatherless sons may struggle to form healthy relationships with peers, family members, and romantic partners, leading to feelings of loneliness and isolation.

Here are the devastating effects of fatherlessness on your son's life:

➤ 85% of youths in prisons grew up in a fatherless home.
➤ 71% of high school dropouts come from fatherless homes.

- ➢ 80% of rapists with displaced anger come from fatherless homes.
- ➢ 63% of youth suicides are from fatherless homes.
- ➢ 90% of homeless children are from fatherless homes.
- ➢ 85% of children with behavioral disorders come from fatherless homes.

In addition, fatherless boys are disproportionately more likely to end up in prison. The prison incarceration rate has more than quadrupled since 2005. With the increase comes sons sharing a prison cell with their father. At Elmira's maximum-security prison in upstate New York are father and son Scott and Bernard Peters. There are many more to come if we don't stop the epidemic.

Gangs and criminal networks are good at satisfying this primal need of belonging. They provide an empty, deceptive disguise of safety, fellowship, and meaning. In principle, they fill those gaps in many disconnected, lonely boys and, in doing so, lead them to a darker sense of purpose.

Some say good men are not born. They are built, shaped, and molded during their childhood and adolescent years by their experiences, influences, communities, and, most importantly, the mentors in their lives that they look up to.

Our boys are crying out. Your son is crying out. They need you to tell them how to walk and live in their manhood. They need you to make them a priority and show them they matter.

If you abandon your kid but choose to raise your other children, you are trash.
If you abandon your child and choose to raise someone else's, your even bigger trash. No child deserves to wonder why they were not enough for a parent who is capable of taking care of other children.

# SEVEN

## MAKING AMENDS

"I'm sorry" - two of the most powerful words known to humanity. These two words, given in love and grace, can make the difference between a life filled with emotional pain and one filled with joy and serenity. It can be both easy and challenging to utter these two words.

What is the difference between amends and apology?

When making amends, you go further than offering an apology. Making amends as an absent father can be a challenging and sensitive process, but it is possible to take steps toward reconciliation and rebuilding relationships with your children. Here are some suggestions on how an absent father can make amends:

1. **Acknowledge the Impact** It's important to acknowledge the impact of your absence on your children. Recognize the hurt, pain, and feelings of abandonment they have experienced because of your absence. Some children have suffered immensely in the absence of an absent father. There are boys and girls in institutions who can attest to this. You may never know all of what they have endured.

2. **Speak positively about their mother**. It is so important **not** to blame the mother, even if she intentionally kept you away from

your child. Trust me, your daughter knows who the guilty parties are.

3. **Apologize** - Offer a sincere apology to your children for not being there for them. **DO NOT MAKE EXCUSES!** Take responsibility for your actions and the consequences of your absence. I'd start with a direct apology. Honest answers. Genuine remorse. They're going to be pissed, probably. But on another level, I am thankful. Never forget you are the guilty party.

4. **Make amends.** Today, children will call bullshit immediately if they sense it. Most times, it is easy to say things—your kids need to see the action behind your apology. You may even try asking your children what they'd like to see from you to amplify your sincerity.

5. **Listen** to your children's feelings, thoughts, and concerns without judgment. Allow them to express how your absence has affected them and be open to understanding their perspective. They are angry, hurt, and possibly in pain.

Let them express themselves freely. In the spirit of honesty, you should be open to accepting feedback from your children. Making amends should be more of a dialogue rather than a monologue, and your children may offer you valuable insights and critiques. Fostering a relationship with your children that invites truthful conversation is wise.

1. **Be Consistent.** Show your commitment to being present in your children's lives moving forward. Consistency is key to

rebuilding trust and showing dedication to being an active and involved parent.

2. **Seek Counseling** Consider seeking the help of a therapist or counselor to work through any underlying issues that may have contributed to your absence. Family therapy can also be beneficial in facilitating communication and healing within the family unit.

3. **Make Time for Your Children** attempt to spend quality time with your children and take part in their lives. Engage in activities together, attend their events, and show your genuine interest in their well-being.

4. **Respect Boundaries** Understand that rebuilding trust takes time and respect your children's boundaries as they navigate their feelings toward you. Be patient and allow them to set the pace for the relationship. Become someone they can talk to, a friend, and then perhaps a parent.

5. **Educate Yourself** Take the time to educate yourself on effective parenting strategies, communication skills, and ways to foster a healthy parent-child relationship. Consider reading books, attending parenting classes, or seeking expert guidance. Educate yourself about your child. Find out as much about her as you can.

6. **Stay Committed** Making amends as an absent father is an ongoing process that requires dedication and effort. Stay committed to your children and continue to show them love, support, and understanding. If you can't visit, call them.

Remember that every situation is unique, and making amends will vary with the dynamics involved. **It's never too late** to take steps towards reconciliation and rebuilding relationships with your children, and with patience, empathy, and effort, you can work towards healing and strengthening your bond with your child.

**What if my child is not receptive to reconnecting?**

If your child is not receptive to reconnecting with you, it can be challenging. However, there are still steps the father can take to work towards reconciliation:

7. **Respect Their Wishes and understand the child may** need more time and space to heal from the past. Respect their boundaries and avoid forcing a relationship if they are not ready.

8. **Be Patient and Persistent.** Rebuilding trust takes time. Continue to express your desire to reconnect, but do so respectfully and non-confrontationally. Let the child know you are available when they are ready.

9. **Seek Mediation.** Consider involving a neutral third party, such as a therapist or counselor, who can facilitate communication and help navigate the reconciliation process. This can create a safe space for the child to express their feelings.

10. **Write Letters or Send Cards.** If direct communication is difficult, consider writing letters or sending cards to your child expressing your regret, love, and commitment to being a better parent. This allows you to share your message

without pressure. We can help you with writing to your child.

11. **Demonstrate Change** Show, over time, your changed behavior and commitment to being a consistently present and supportive parent through your actions. This can include attending important events, being reliable, and showing genuine interest in the child's life.

12. **Seek Counseling Yourself.** Work on your personal growth and healing. Seek counseling to address any issues that may have contributed to your absence, such as mental health challenges, addiction, or relationship difficulties. This can help you become a healthier and more present parent.

13. **Respect Their Decision.** If, despite your efforts, the child remains unwilling to reconnect, respect their decision. Understand that the child has the right to choose when or if they are ready to have a relationship with you. At the end of the day, what matters is that you can honestly say you tried.

The most important thing is approaching the situation with **empathy, patience**, and a genuine **desire** to make amends. Rebuilding trust and a relationship takes time, and the child's needs and emotional well-being should be the top priority.

> "Denying, or attempting to deny, a child the joy and memories that come with being with the other parent is unequivocally an act of evil"

# EIGHT

## PARENTAL ALIENATION

*Being a mother is a role that involves caring for and nurturing a child and providing love, support, and guidance. It can also mean taking on several roles, including protector, friend, teacher, and role model.*

One of my childhood friends always wanted to be a police officer and when he became one, the community celebrated him and his family. His dream had come true, and we were proud of him. We knew what type of police officer he was going to be.

Approximately five years after joining the force, the same neighborhood that celebrated him watched the evening news in shock and disgust as officers led him out of his parent's house in handcuffs, charging him with sexual abuse of a minor. He was on all the networks.

The minor he allegedly sexually assaulted was his six-year-old daughter, a child he adored, worshipped, and protected. The person accusing him was the child's mother, his ex-girlfriend. Three months after their six-year relationship ended, his ex-girlfriend made the accusation.

Public disclosure of the sordid details cost him his job and standing in the community; he lost his home, cars, and almost everything of value. His parents lost their retirement and several rental properties to cover his legal fees. They labeled him a pedophile before his arraignment. Even people who knew him from childhood shunned him.

Fast forward one year and one week before his trial, the district attorney announced at a press conference that he had dropped all charges.

The ex-girlfriend admitted he did not harm his daughter and stated she tells the story of abuse to keep him away from his daughter because "he had a new girlfriend" There was no apology from the district attorney or his baby's mother. The damage was done.

He was a broken man with a shattered dream. Despite his exoneration, no law enforcement agency employed him. More importantly, he lost precious time with his daughter. It took years of therapy for his daughter to grasp her father wasn't the monster in the closet or under the bed. The actual monster was the one putting her to bed and kissing her good night.

My friend is but one of thousands of men from all walks of life who experienced the loss of a relationship with their child at the expense of a vindictive mother.

I believe mothers are complicit in and accountable for any trauma or pain their children endure when travesties of justice like this happen. To voluntarily inflict and expose such trauma on your child to harm another person, you must be some kind of evil or sick individual.

Parental Alienation, or Parental Alienation Syndrome, describes a mother's behavior of keeping a child away from his or her father.

**What is Parental Alienation?**

People also call parental alienation parental alienation syndrome.

Parental alienation is the process where one parent (alienating parent) negatively influences their child's (alienated child) relationship with the other parent (targeted/alienated parent).

It occurs when one parent attempts to discourage their child from having contact with the other parent without reasonable justification. And this can happen even when the child and targeted parent used to have a very positive and close relationship.

This shows that parental alienation is not only a form of psychological child abuse. But that it's also abuse towards the targeted parent.

Although we use the term "parent", alienating or targeted individuals are not always mothers or fathers. It can also be a grandparent, stepparent, sibling, or non-family member.

**10 Signs of Parental Alienation**

Here are some signs, examples, and behaviors to see whether your ex-partner was an alienating parent.

One common sign of parental alienation is when the alienating parent often denigrates the other parent to the child.

Your alienating parent may name-call, insult, make implications, or make backhanded compliments about your other parent.

They may also refuse to use the other parent's name and acknowledge anything good about them.

**Accusing the other parent of abuse**

The alienating parent may claim or imply that the other parent is abusive without reason or evidence. They can take an innocent or normal situation and twist it into something sinister.

For instance, if the other parent was helping their child change or bathe, the alienating parent may accuse them of sexual abuse.

Or if the other parent says "no" to the child or asks them to do something, the alienating parent may claim they're being controlling or emotionally abusive.

Also, if a child is reluctant to or avoids contact with the other parent, the alienating parent would use that as "evidence" of wrongdoing by the other parent.

For example, here is what alienating parents might do to get the targeted parent in trouble:

- ➢ Call Child Protective Services to report the other parent for abuse.
- ➢ File for a restraining order on the other parent.
- ➢ Go to a professional to claim the other parent is abusive.

➢ Reach out to organizations for "help" on an abusive partner or ex.

**Forcing the child's loyalty to them**

Alienating parents expect their children to be completely loyal to them.

The alienating parent may pressure or even force the child to take their side whenever there's any conflict.

Someone forbids the child from showing prejudice or preference to either parent. The alienating parent might also try to guilt-trip the child to their side.

Whenever the child wants to spend time with the other parent, the alienating parent may interfere. They may schedule a better activity or event, so they choose to spend time with them instead.

Or they may call or text non-stop while the child is with the other parent, so the child can't enjoy their time with them.

The alienating parent might do many things, some of which can be extremely petty, just to keep you from spending time or bonding with the father.

The alienating parent may also intentionally prevent the child from spending time with family and friends. And to truly try to eradicate the other parent's existence in the child's life, the alienating parent may even act like they don't exist at all. Or they may have even tried to get someone else to replace them like a new partner whom they try to get the child to call "Dad."

**Encouraging an unhealthy bond with the child**

The alienating parent may encourage their child to depend on them. They may have the child believe they can't function without them.

It may also be the other way around where they may rely on the child and claim they can't be happy without the child in their life. This is also known as **emotional incest**, where the parent makes the child their surrogate spouse.

In this relationship, the parent turns to the child for emotional support. The child is expected to meet the parent's needs, including going against the other parent to "protect" this one.

We also term this unhealthy bond, characterized by overlapping and blurred personal boundaries between parent and child enmeshment.

In an enmeshed relationship, the parent and child cannot separate their emotional experiences from each other. They usually become so overly involved in each other's lives that they lose their autonomy.

**Effects of Parental Alienation on the Alienated Child**

Many researchers consider parental alienation to be a form of psychological child abuse. However, some argue it's just "parental conflict" or the child's "conflicting loyalties."

Though that may be the case, a parent's active participation in turning their child against the other parent *is* abuse because of the harmful effects it leaves on the child.

Children who have experienced parental alienation are at a higher risk of disorders such as;

- Depression
- Anxiety
- Eating disorders and body image issues
- Addiction and substance use
- Post-traumatic stress disorder
- Other mental and psychosomatic disorders
- Damage to the parent-child and other relationships

In severe cases, there is often long-term or even permanent damage to the relationship and contact between the child and the targeted parent. This may also affect siblings as well.

By alienating the child, the child doesn't get what might otherwise be a healthy and meaningful parent-child relationship. The child may also miss out on relationships with extended family members on that parent's side. They may also miss out on certain childhood experiences, activities, and other relationships essential for healthy development.

Because of parental alienation, the child lost what could've been a significant support for their growth and development. Meanwhile, they get riddled with various effects left by this form of abuse instead.

**Damaged or a loss of a sense of self**

Parental alienation can have serious negative effects on the child's psychological welfare. It can change their perceptions, not just of the targeted parent, but of themselves.

According to the research, "the imposed, active rejection, denial, and reality-distorting image of a previously loved parent is damaging to the child's self and core." It might cause severe feelings of guilt or even self-hatred in the child.

The child may internalize their hatred or rejection of the targeted parent. Or they may believe their targeted parent didn't love or want them.

They may also forget how to trust their own feelings and perceptions because they've depended on the alienating parent on what to believe and think.

All of this may also cause self-isolation, shame, insecurity, low self-worth, and low self-esteem.

Here are some other effects of parental alienation according to the latest research:

- Future relationship problems and difficulties
- Possibility of becoming targeted/alienated parents
- Personality difficulties
- ADHD
- Self-harm
- Suicidal ideation

- Helplessness
- Feelings of grief and loss
- Feelings of anger
- Trust issues
- Feelings of abandonment
- Maladaptive coping
- Confusion about their experience
- Reduced or delayed educational and career attainment

One day you're going to wake up and notice that you should've tried.

I was worth the fight.

# NINE

## ON THEIR BEHALF

*"What is done to our children, they will do to society."*
**Karl Menninger, MD**

There is nothing more painful than having a fifteen-year-old girl cry on your shoulder as she asks what's wrong with her, why isn't she loved, or what she did wrong for her father not to love her. I have wiped the eyes of too many of those heartbroken girls.

There is nothing more gut-wrenching than watching a boy who has been labeled a thug and a horrible human express his anger, pain, and frustration but cannot articulate why he is so angry, which we know will ultimately further his problems and a future in the legal system.

We all are complicit in not holding the absent fathers in our circles accountable. That has to change. Society and communities are being decimated because of broken children. Babies are being born to broken children.

At the same time, their absent fathers look away and live their best lives or blame a system or ideology or their child's mother.

The absent fathers are our pastors, brothers, uncles, nephews, cousins, and neighbors. They are in our churches, workplaces, and fraternities. We golf, play tennis, and basketball with these fathers, yet we don't inquire about their broken children. We see them at funerals, reunions, and social functions with their new families, and we say nothing—it is complicity at its finest.

We should view fatherlessness as a psychological trauma that deserves special attention and care because of its societal impact. If not, we will soon see another society of broken adults.

In the '70s, there was a men's club in Houston, Texas, named the White Rose. It was owned and tightly managed by a gentleman named Mr. Jonas. The club was a safe space for high-rollers who gambled, stick-up men, pimps, and other members of the criminal community. My father and uncle were well-known, long-standing members.

Despite the club's criminal element, it had unwritten rules regarding families of members. If there was beef between members, their families were off-limits. Mr. Jonas, despite his business, was a family man known for supporting families in the community.

Another rule of the club was that if a gambler lost his money, which was meant for groceries or rent, and asked the house to borrow money for said items, that was a major problem with dire consequences besides the high-interest loan.

One day, while picking up my father's winnings to take to my mother, I watched a man in the rear of the club get jumped.

I later learned that he had lost a sizable amount of money meant for his mortgage and groceries and had no choice but to ask the house for a loan.

Now, I don't believe we should physically assault absent fathers, but they do not deserve a pass. We can and should call them out and not give them a safe space. We must hold absent fathers accountable for their children's suffering. As a society, we must do whatever we can to save our children because they matter.

Finally, absent fathers, I hope this book has encouraged or motivated you to connect emotionally with your child. If you want to reach out to your child but don't know what to say or how to express your feelings, we can help. Email us (serenityobtained@gmail.com) and let us know what you would like to do, and we will do our best to assist you.

If you choose not to heed the message of this book, the last chapter contains letters children and adults have written to their absent fathers—you do not want to receive or be the subject of one of these letters. I wish you well.

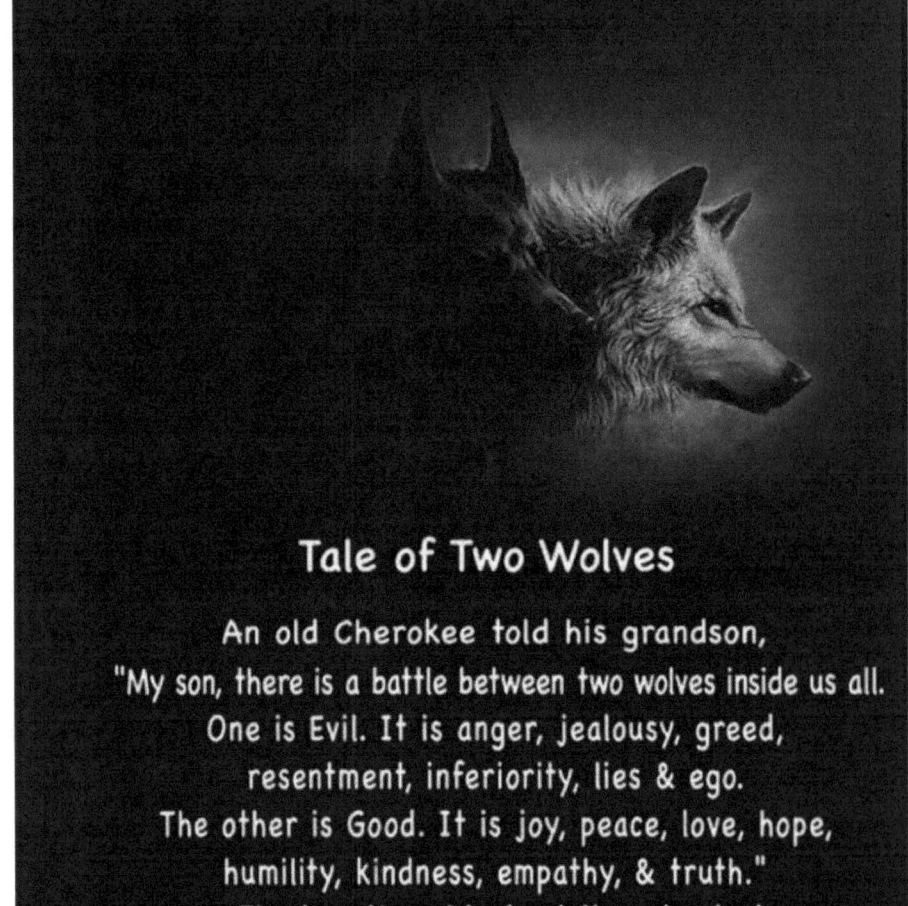

## Tale of Two Wolves

An old Cherokee told his grandson,
"My son, there is a battle between two wolves inside us all.
One is Evil. It is anger, jealousy, greed,
resentment, inferiority, lies & ego.
The other is Good. It is joy, peace, love, hope,
humility, kindness, empathy, & truth."
The boy thought about it, and asked,
"Grandfather, which wolf wins?"
The old man quietly replied,
"The one you feed."

# TEN

## ONE LAST THING

Many years ago, I took six teenage boys from the neighborhood on a road trip. The purpose of the trip was for them to see another view of life and less concrete. Only one had a father in the home, and it was a chaotic relationship because the father was an addict. However, I didn't take them because of their absent fathers. I took care of them because I knew their parents and I cared for them as though they were my children. I felt I had an obligation to uplift the community.

We had conversations about sex, violence in the hood, education, and our dreams during our 100-plus-mile trip. They questioned me about my fears, my relationship with my father, and how to approach a potential employer. I was vulnerable and brutally honest with them. When I told them I feared ducks, there wasn't a dry eye in the car. If they saw a duck on clothing or a picture, they made me regret sharing my fears. It was the only time I regretted bringing their little asses on the trip.

They had known me most of their life, so they knew I would keep it real with them.

Now, here is the thing: 30-plus years later, these same young men with children of their own still talk about the trip, the restaurants we ate at, and the stores we shopped in. They even remembered some conversations we had and asked when we would do it again. And yes, they brought up the ducks.

Men, we have what it takes to be what our sons and daughters need. Did you know men produce in great quantity a hormone called vasopressin? Vasopressin is the protective, aggressive hormone that helps fathers protect their families.

I say to the big homies, absent fathers, grandfathers, uncles, cousins, family friends–our boys need you desperately.

Meet them with grace and no strings attached, and watch a miracle appear before you. They don't need your money or a lot of your time. They need your presence now and then to remind them they are protected and matter to someone.

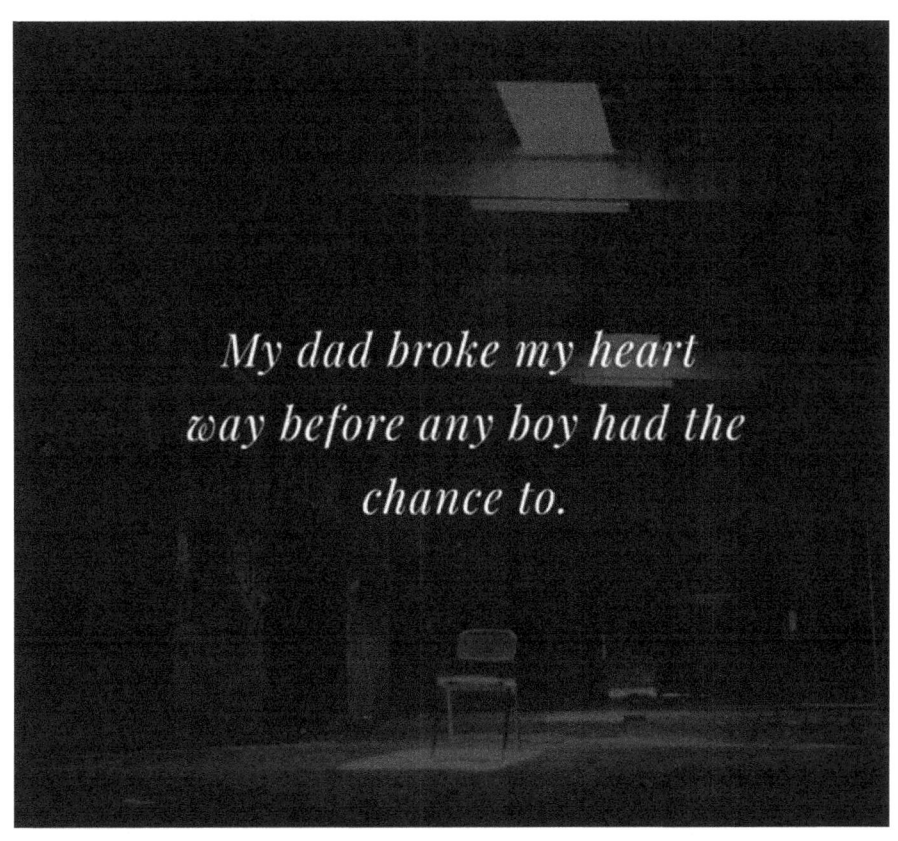

# ELEVEN

## LETTERS TO MY FATHER

As I mentioned earlier, I put out a call to children of abandoned fathers and asked them to share a thought, quote, or letter about the impact of their absent fathers. My request resonated deeply with many men and women. Countless women and men shared their ongoing struggles with the pain of their father's abandonment. They also showed the power of journaling and writing.

Make copies of these unedited letters and share them with a father you know who is no longer in touch with his son or daughter. However, he would like to be in contact with them one day.

Perhaps these letters will give him hope and motivate him to change the narrative. Also, share this letter with a woman who has negative feelings towards her dad and is ready to address her abandonment issues and low self-worth or a son who can't get past his anger of abandonment.

May these letters facilitate dialogue, healing, tranquility, and reconciliation between fathers and their abandoned children.

*Dear absent fathers,*

*Your children don't have the ability to articulate their feelings and as someone who was abandoned by her father, I'm here as their voice. This letter is not written to shame you, it's written out of love. A love from a daughter to her father that doesn't even know her.*

*I'm writing to let you know that your children still need you. Perhaps you've moved on to a new family or to a new life. Maybe you feel that your children have got a good mother and you're thinking to yourself, "She'll take care of them. They don't need me." Maybe in some way you have justified that moving on and leaving them with their mother, perhaps even a new stepfather, would be better for your children.*

**Well, you're wrong. Your children DO need you.**

*And they always will. My father abandoned my sister and me as preschoolers. We saw him on and off for a few years. A few hours here and there over the years. Just like approximately thirty percent of children of divorce, my parents' separation meant a permanent separation between us and our father. Now, as an adult woman who hasn't seen her father in over 25 years, there's still an emptiness in my heart.*

*Like the other three in ten children of fathers who abandoned their children, I contemplated suicide as a young person. I questioned whether I was worthy of love. Deep rooted feelings of unworthiness and doubts still haunt me from my childhood. If my own father doesn't love me, how could another man? I pray that your children will never question the love you have for them or whether they are worthy of love at all.*

*Perhaps your ex-wife is making things difficult. She hates you and she's poisoning your children against you. She tells you that the children hate you and don't want to see you. You don't want to deal with the drama and the negativity.* **Deal with it**. *Your children are worth it. They want you to fight for them. If dealing with their 'horrible' mother is the price to pay for spending time with them, then, dammit, they are worth it. In the long run, when you have a rewarding relationship with your children, you'll be glad you endured.*

**Maybe somewhere in your head, you've rationalized that your children are better off without you.**

*But when the dust settles and the divorce is behind you, your children will still love their father and seek love from you. Right now, they may be lashing out. They feel the anger and the bitterness of divorce-only they lack the tools and maturity to understand it. Be patient. It may take time for them to come around. Be there for them when they mature enough that they are ready for a relationship with you.*

*Stay open and available to them. Let the barbs and stings that they throw at you make you stronger for them. If you give up and allow the negativity to win, your children will lose. They'll wonder why you didn't fight for them. Always reach out and say that you are there for them when they are ready.*

*Find the support and resources you need to navigate this process. Help is out there. If you want to build your relationship with your children, find a counsellor or a divorce coach to support you through the process. Do what is needed, sacrifice your ego, and find your way to them. Give your children the unconditional love of a father. You'll never regret it. Abandoned Daughter (64 years old)*

*DearDad,*

*How are you? It's been awhile. Or for some of us, it's never been. We are women now. You've missed a lot. You missed so many important moments in our lives. Where do we start? Our birth? When you found out mom was pregnant, you couldn't handle it. You didn't know what to do. You may have been too young. You may not have had a father figure, so you didn't know how to be a father. Who knows. Some of you stayed in the picture a little longer. You stayed a few years after I was born. At first, things were great. You and mom got along. Maybe you thought having me would help. Maybe you thought sticking it out would help. Things got tough. You began to fight with mom. You may have lost your job. You may have had a great job, perhaps the stressors of home got to you. We will never know. What we do know is what you missed when you walked out that door. You missed the numerous first days of school. You missed Back to School nights and Open Houses. You missed Girl Scouts, sports, dance recitals, holidays, summers, vacations, first dates, graduations and college acceptance letters. You missed romantic relationships, weddings, birth of your grandchild, job promotions, etc. The fun and exciting stuff.*

*You also missed the not-so-exciting stuff. When you left and didn't pay child support, we had to move out of our home and collect financial assistance. We had to shop at Goodwill because mom could not afford clothing. We had to grow up fast. We had to take care of our younger siblings. We had to be emotional support for our mothers. Whatever childhood we had, was gone. We had to listen to mom cry herself to sleep. We saw her date men who were not good to her, or good to us. We needed to start working at 16 because money was a little tight. Sometimes we missed out on parties and school events to work because we needed to make sure the lights stayed on and food was on the table. We started looking for attention outside the home. We wanted love and affection that we did not get from you, so we started looking in other places. Friends, partners, drugs/alcohol, crime, teen pregnancy or food. Many times we found it in men. To be honest, the men did not treat us well at all. However, we didn't care. It was a man. It was someone that held us (sometimes), was by our side (sometimes), called us (sometimes), told us they loved us (sometimes), married us, or had a child with us. We didn't care, we just wanted someone to be there and tell us they loved us because you weren't there. Although their love was sporadic and contingent, at least it was there.*

*We can honestly say your leaving really affected our self-esteem and self-worth. We don't feel good about ourselves at all. We don't feel that we are good enough for any man, partner, friend, or career. We don't feel lovable. We feel like a disappointment. We feel we don't belong.*

*When you left we felt so many negative feelings. We realize those feelings are still there. Anger, resentment, sadness, grief, shame, fear, guilt, doubt, and betrayal. We are trying to work through these feelings through therapy. We realize holding on to these feelings no longer serves us. They are causing us to hate ourselves.*

*We love everyone else more than we love ourselves. We are ready to love ourselves. We are ready to look deep inside ourselves to see how our life has been affected by you leaving. We are not here to blame. We are women now. We cannot blame you because we stayed with partners that don't treat us right. We cannot blame you for our lack of confidence in going for the job we want. Our childhood circumstances were not our fault. We were thrown into a situation that affected the way we looked at life and interacted with the world. We are ready to take responsibility for our choices in adulthood. We made the choices that reflected how we felt about ourselves. Our past does not have to define our future. We are beginning to realize:*

WE ARE ENOUGH!
WE ARE LOVEABLE!
WE BELONG!
WE ARE SUCCESSFUL!

*We get to feel joy, peace, happiness, courage, confidence, acceptance, hopeful, love and trust.*

*At this point, We no longer care why you left. We can no longer hold on to that story. We are ready to write a new story. If you would like to be in it, and if you would like to rewrite your own story, contact us. You had your own story and that is why you left. We get that now. We have learned it was never about us. You left not because there was something wrong with us, but it was something up with you. We see that now.*

*Happy Father's Day!*

*Dear dad,*

*I guess you do know who I am; I had half hoped you had forgotten me. In all these years, that was the thought that hurt the least. The reality is that you don't want anything to do with me. I got it now.*

*Where were you when my mother died? I was barely ten and had no one. I had to take care of myself in a place with people who had never cared for me and treated me so badly that I questioned my own existence. You made a choice for which I suffered intensely. I've let it go, but trust me, I'll never forget.*

*I still question why my mother never taught me to hate you. You were worthy of my hate. Mom was always happy when she talked about you, even though you caused her such pain. I don't know what happened, but one day, I found her dead, and suddenly, my world became small and empty. I was alone.*

*So many things happened around me and on a daily basis that I'm starting to believe I'm cursed. The basis of my being has been shaken, and I am no longer safe around the people I care about. Calling you last night was a mistake because you showed me that you would never be my refuge, my sanctuary of peace. I am without.*

*I miss the father I imagined you to be, the father you never were. One day, my dear father, you'll wake up and notice that you should have tried because I was worth the fight. Be well. Ayn*

*Dear Dad,*

*Did you even want me? When you held me for the first time, did you plan on tossing me aside like garbage?*

*Up until I was twelve, I was a Daddy's girl, of course, you know that, but that all changed when you abandoned me…when you threw me to the side after the divorce.*

*We used to have daddy-daughter dates. Remember when you, Marilyn, and I went to the arcades every other weekend? I was utterly devastated when you took that time away. Learning that you'd rather spend ALL of your time with women you met online instead of with your child damaged the relationship I had with you.*

*I would never understand why you ignored me…snubbed me. How can your own flesh and blood be replaced by the hoes you met online? Back then, you spent all your time and money caring for them…charming them on our daddy-daughter dates. This consumed all of you, leaving me abandoned by you emotionally, physically, and financially.*

*If you are my father, then how on earth could you abandon me?*

*How could you not consistently pay child support for eight years but yet lay up in your house taking care of women and feeding their kids?*

*If you are my father, why do you not support me? So many nights, we had to eat Ramen noodles for dinner, miss payments on our bills, and forego new experiences all because you thought Mom could handle being both the provider and caretaker…being both mother and father to Bailey and me. As wonderful as she is, Mom was excellent at wearing both hats, but I needed you.*

*For eight years, I needed you. I needed you to teach me how to drive, watch me try on dresses for prom, and help me find the right college to apply to. More simply, I needed you to come and cheer me on at my volleyball games. All I needed for you to do was come and support me during my volleyball career. You had the chance to come to all those games, but you decided otherwise. You decided that I was not important.*

*For eight years, I needed you to love me.*

*You weren't there for so much of my life; my friends started to think that I did not have a birth father at all. 80% of the people in my life barely know your name, let alone what you look like.*

*I always hoped that you would wake up one day and realize how horrible you are for ditching your kids. The little piece of hope I carried in my inconsolable heart was quickly squashed when Facebook told me that you got engaged. I found out through Facebook! Do you know how horrible that was for me?*

*Regrettably, I was surrounded by my teammates on an overnight trip when I saw the announcement on my feed. That day, I had to explain to my teammates why I was morbidly crying in the bathroom.*

*You continue to blame me for all this sorrow I have about you being absent in my life. You say it is my fault that we don't have a relationship. I should call you. I have a car, so I should drive to your house. The last time I checked, you abandoned me, so why should I, the victim, run to someone who never aspired to be a father? I hate how you invalidate my feelings.*

*Even though I don't like what you did and how you disregarded your responsibilities, I still love you. I am still that little girl wishing for her father to take her on daddy-daughter dates.*

*Your impact, small or large, on my life hasn't turned my whole world into darkness. While your negligence has caused me much pain, I turned out to be a resilient young woman who is benevolent, independent, strong, and unconfined. I am still working through the emotional impact of your absence, but in time, I will heal and learn to put the past behind me.*

*Your Daughter, Megan*

*Dear Tre',*

*When I had the idea to write this letter, I could think of a million things I could write. But now that I'm actually doing it, I'm at a loss for words.*

*I deserve so much better than you. I deserve a father who demonstrates his love for me through actions and effort, not just $100 on my birthday and Christmas. That always hurt me, by the way. Just giving me cash because you never knew me well enough even to know what I liked, and the attempt and interest in learning more was never there.*

*Your conditional love has destroyed me. Your selfishness has never ceased to amaze me. And, whenever I thought you couldn't get any worse, you somehow always did.*

*You always did your best to ensure I knew how disappointed you were in me and how I was doing a bad job maintaining our relationship. It didn't matter to you that I was a child. All that mattered was that I was responsible for making sure you had all your needs met and were happy.*

*I despise you. For as long as I can remember, you have done nothing but break my heart. And for so long, you convinced me that it was my fault. Mom and I were always the villains; it could never be you.*

*Because it was your world, and we were living in it. I also want you to know that I have a hard time referring to you as my dad. For the past few years, you have been reduced to sperm donor because, as far as I'm concerned, the most you have ever done for me was create half of my DNA.*

*Since then, you have been virtually useless to me, as I have been made to feel I have been to you, too.*

*I hate you. I hate the way you've treated me my entire life. The way you've manipulated me, the way you've hurt me over and over again, the way your love was always conditional. I hate how you talked about and treated my mom. She is the best person I know and deserves the world. What she didn't deserve was you. Selfish, unfaithful, flaky, manipulative, awful you. I would not wish you upon my worst enemy.*

*I feel sorry for you, though, because you do not have the privilege of seeing and knowing who I've become, the woman my mother raised. I am smart, kind, funny, and talented—no thanks to you. I am a college graduate with dreams and goals that I will someday achieve because I know I have what it takes to be resilient—I get that from her.*

*I want to thank you for something, though, that is showing me your true colors. I am so glad I know exactly what I never hoped to become. You may be half my DNA, but I will never be anything like you.*

*All the missed dance competitions, parent/teacher conferences, shows, ceremonies, concerts, and general life milestones have been a loss on your part, not mine. You are the one with the void, not me. And even though you have done nothing but hurt me for as long as I can remember, it's you for whom I feel sorry.*

*I feel nothing but disgust for you. You will never be my dad — just some coward who ran off and left his baby girl to wonder why she wasn't worth it for you to stay.*

*I hope you're living the life you deserve.* Cheryl

*The One Who Walked Away: A Letter to My Absent Father*

*There are videos of me at a very young age, asking why "that man" was in our home.*

*That man is my father.*

*You see when you grow up and someone is hardly around, it's hard to remember that they hold any sort of significance in your life. I spent the beginning of my childhood with just my mom as an only child. Once my brother was born in 1994, I went from feeling scared and alone to being empowered and knowing I had to protect him. This is my letter to my absent father for Father's Day:*

*Dear...Dad?*

*I'm unsure how to address you anymore, as it's been well over a year since I last saw you. Even before that, things were not great. This is not the first time I have written you a letter. In fact, the last letter gave my mom the voice she needed to go through the divorce. It was easier to write down all of my thoughts because you were never around for me to argue with.*

*In my younger years, you continuously had excuses for why you were gone. I distinctly remember you walking out of my eighth-grade graduation dinner because you raced that night. For whatever reason, driving a race car was more important than my childhood.*

*That car took you all over Iowa, sometimes resulting in you being gone for multiple weekends in a row. If it wasn't the car, it was your job. You'd conveniently take a two-week+ assignment to work on building homes. Anywhere but here.*

*The times you actually were home, I resented you even more as you sat in the basement, smoking one cigarette after another. Our entire home reeked of smoke, and I would lie angrily in my bed each night, forced to inhale the smell until I fell asleep.*

*The best part about you finally moving out was that we could breathe fresh air in our own home for the first time.*

*When the divorce was final, I was eighteen years old and away at college. It was hard for Mom to raise two kids independently, but it was better than the alternative.*

*I never understood the point of being married to someone who was never present. I missed games and school programs, and I could not even know our simple likes and dislikes.*

*Was there truly a point in keeping this person around?*

*After that, you'd pop in occasionally, usually around our birthdays and Christmas. For years, we'd hide when you came to the door as if you were a salesperson soliciting the neighborhood. Even as an adult, when you only see someone once or twice a year, it's hard to gather the will to have a quick conversation.*

*I had my twins at twenty, and you found out days later. Your relationship with them was always strange because you'd sign cards, "Love, Grandpa," but never put effort into knowing them.*

*A situation that felt all too familiar.*

*I've spent the majority of my thirty-one years wondering why I was never good enough for you. Why did my father choose his hobbies over being my parent? I've had friends whose fathers passed away, and mine walked out willingly.*

*I have three children now, but maybe you already know that. My youngest looks just like me and has brought so much joy into our lives. I will never allow you to take that away or hurt us more than you already have.*

*I married a man who is the complete opposite of you.*

*My husband is working hard in his career but chose a shift that works best for our family. He's home for dinner every evening and attends every activity he can for the kids. He is my partner and the best father to these three.*

*I owe it to him and myself to let go of the resentment I've held towards you for all these years. I could spend hours debating how someone could ever choose a life without their kids and grandkids, but I'll never find a suitable answer.*

*This Father's Day, I will smile and celebrate my husband. This day is about the dads who stuck around, not the ones who walked away.*

*You will no longer affect how I live or think of myself. I lived with guilt, depression, and a lack of self-worth for too long.*

*Every day, I witness how a father should treat his family and how a man should treat his wife. I'm learning how to fight fairly and that he isn't going to give up on us because something better will come along.*

*Happy Father's Day to my wonderful husband, grandfather, and the fantastic men out there fighting the good fight and being the man their wives and children deserve.*

*Jasmine B.*

*"Sorry" is a word frequently used in this world. So common, in fact, that unless actions back it up, it's practically useless. I believe forgiveness is divine, but I struggle with bestowing that upon you in particular, my daughter's often-absent father.*

*I don't wish you any ill will. In fact, I hope you lead a happy, fulfilled life. I once cared for you very much. Enough to take on your last name, your questionable past, and the burden of a complicated future. I even went so far as to have a child with you.*

*I don't hate you at all. I just wish you would take the time to include your daughter.*

*To be honest, I'm the one who is sorry.*

*I'm sorry you don't see how beautiful she is in person. Sure you see the pictures I text, but even those can't touch it. You have no idea just how lovely that little girl is.*

*It's simply not enough to call only on a couple major holidays, when you need something, or when it's convenient to you. I even bit my tongue when Christmas came and went with no phone call or present from you. She didn't really notice, but that innocence won't last forever.*

*And yes, she absolutely has the support of her stepfather and extended family, but a little girl likes to know her biological father loves her and thinks about her every day, too. She needs to hear it often and to be shown with actions and effort.*

*You two share the same smirk and hair color, but wouldn't you like to share memories too? Or the inside jokes and humor that fathers and daughters enjoy? You can't name her teacher, best friend, favorite food, favorite color, biggest fear or greatest joy. You're missing out on so much, and I don't think you even realize it. For that, I am truly sorry for you.*

*Always know that she will be ok. We've got this. She has an extended family who love and look out for her, so she will always be cared for. But also know that a day will come when she asks the difficult questions.*

*I hope you have answers. I dread that day because although I relate to her feelings, I don't know what I'll tell her. I worry that I can't possibly be able to ease her mind and heal the hurt.*

*In the end, while she hurts, you're the one truly missing out. She's a beautiful, whip smart young lady who deserves a trip to the moon and stars and everything in between.*

*I'm very sorry you can't experience the privilege of taking that journey with her. You'll realize this one day, and it will surely break your sorry heart.*

*Nicole*

*Dear Dad,*

*You and my mother divorced when I was a toddler and I never developed any childhood memories of you. My mother moved on and married again (four more times, actually). My step-fathers were never really father figures and always seemed like outsiders that never really took ownership of me.*

*Growing up as a boy, I longed to have you in my life and as I grew older I became more aware of a deep-seeded hurt and frustration. I had a lot of questions and judgmental thoughts that ran through my mind, especially when Father's Day came.*

*In my twenties, I tried to be very busy on Father's Day because if I stopped and thought about it too long I could bring myself to tears with questions of "Why?"*

*Now I am in the latter half of my thirties and I am a father to a son of my own. I have noticed that since becoming a father, Father's Day has taken on a new meaning. I have also noticed that the last couple of years I have not ruminated on your sins against me.*

*This year, I made a decision that I have forgiven you—I have let it go. I sometimes wonder if other men and women with absent fathers like you have ever looked for reasons to move on. I wanted to share with you why I am choosing to move on.*

*You were not a bad father. For years, all I could think was that you did not want me and that if you were around at least you could teach me something. You could play catch with me.*

*You could help me figure out how to talk to the pretty girl in class. You could tell me that my first wet dream was normal. You could explain how to hide an erection in the fifth grade when I had to get up in front of class and write out a math problem on the board.*

*The last couple of years I have seen the other side of the coin. In other words, I may have missed out on the positive aspects of having a father around, but I also missed out on the negative aspects of having a father around.*

*I was not raised with the influence of a father that was a womanizer, an abuser, or an addict—-though you may have been any or all of those things.*

*By your absence I was spared learning a template of what a father was but shouldn't be. I could draw a parallel with you being an absentee father and others who lost their fathers in accidents or wars. I*

*n short, not having a father is probably better than having a bad father. So, I choose to let your absence go.*

*I learned how important a father is. I went to Boy Scout campouts alone. I never had a dad on the sideline of the soccer field coaching me or cheering me on. I never got to skip school for a surprise father-son day.*

*On my wedding day, you weren't there to tell me not to wear a banana hammock under my suit on the way to the honeymoon. You* weren't there to help me deal with our first miscarriage. I worried whether I would ever be a father after our second and third miscarriages; I wondered what you would say if you were there.

All of these situations have proven to me how valuable a father's love, encouragement, and wisdom can be in the everyday moments of life.

My conviction, my mission, to be a nurturing father fuels anger when I come across fathers who are so casual about their parenting responsibilities, so dismissive of their opportunities to connect with their children.

Your absence has made my hearing very sensitive to the calling I have as an active and responsible parent. So, I choose to let your absence go.

Insecurity has motivated me to push myself and find myself. Because you were not there to help figure out what it means to be a man, for a long time I questioned whether or not I was doing this man-thing right.

There was a void in my identity and I was quick to compare myself to other men and either be critical of them or too hard on myself.

I pushed myself to accomplish goals in spite of your absence. I was the first to graduate high school the traditional way by walking at a graduation ceremony; I was the only one to join the military; I was the first to graduate college.

Somewhere along this journey, I realized that it was okay to be a good man and a good father, even if I didn't get to see you be one.

*Over the years, I have come to the conclusion that being a man to me means the pursuit of integrity and having accountability with my relationships.*

*In hindsight, typing these words seems ironic as I set out to be exactly what I thought I needed from you. I now realize that I was expecting something from you that you did not have to give. So, I choose to let your absence go.*

*By no means am I grateful to you for being absent. I am not. And, my choice to forgive is not because I no longer feel pain, or because I am justifying your choices. I grieve that I did not have a father growing up. Sometimes, I still grieve about you not being in my life now.*

*It's taken me years to realize, but now I know that I am not really grieving the loss of our relationship or the loss of your love. What I am really grieving is the loss of the father in my mind (and that is the father I now try to be to my child), not the person that you actually are. That may sound harsh, but I think it is the truth.*

*I want you to know where ever you are that I choose to let go of your sins against me, of being absent. I think it may have inadvertently made me stronger and more attentive as a man, a husband, and a father.*

Letting You Go

*I don't hate you.*

*I used to. I used to wish I'd open the paper and find that you'd overdosed or been killed. I held so much hate inside of me that I couldn't see anything else except the bad that you had done.*

*I used to find myself up at 3am, breast feeding my son, thinking of how you were most likely partying, or taking care of another woman's children, and I felt rage inside of myself.*

*I was so blinded by this rage that I couldn't do anything else except hate you. I wasn't mad for what WE weren't; I was mad for my son, and let me tell you, there is no feeling that can mirror a mother's rage when someone has wronged their child.*

*I don't know exactly when this stopped. I can't pinpoint a specific day or a certain event where I just stopped hating you. It was a mixture of events and days that blurred together out of exhaustion, that lead to me pitying you, and then to me forgiving you. People listen to my story and they think I'm crazy.*

*After all, I left you, I CHOSE to end us, but you're the one who abandoned our son. You're the one who never tried to be a father. And one day, I just realized that I pity you. I got to see his first everything.*

*I'm the one he cries for when he's hurt. I'm the one he cooed at 2 in the morning when he would wake up to eat.*

*He runs to me when he falls down at the playground, he runs to me when I pick him up from daycare, and he screams to me that he loves me every day. He sings to me and tells me I'm his best friend. I was at the hospital when he had surgery, and I taught him how to do pee pee standing up at the potty.*

*You're missing all of it. And I pity you. You don't even understand how sweet he is, and how loving he is. He is the most caring person, and let's face it, he gets it from my side. From you he has the cutest button nose & big puppy eyes.*

*Then my pity shifted into forgiveness. I forgive the fact that I'm alone raising him. He has turned out to be what has saved my life. I was forced to grow up and to get my shit together. I was thrown into a world where I was up 20 hours out of 24, where I was ecstatic about a new sippy cup purchase, and where I HAD to make plans for my future. I forgive the fact that you're a shitty person, because it's made me a better mother. I love him twice as hard and I will give double that to make up for everywhere you lack.*

*Everyday I wake up and look forward to bettering myself for him. I have something to look forward to because of him, and he has an entire life ahead of him with endless possibilities and limited disappointment because of your absence.*

*I feel sad for the inevitable feelings of sadness and doubt that he will have about himself because of you. My only goal is for him to have a happy life, and I don't think I could've given him that if you were part of it.*

*You will never better yourself. You will never amount to anything. You'll will always be wishing and hoping for something better, and it will never come. You know this, and I know it's part of the reason you stay away.*

*Valerie*

*To My Baby's Father*

*When you pressed send that night, you ended our relationship so casually and so callously. In the time since, my hours have been consumed trying to separate the you I knew, or thought I knew, with the decision you took to close the door on myself and our unborn child so decidedly.*

*I don't know what led you there, the thought processes meandering through your head like tributaries to the ocean, all taking us to the final fact: your absence. I won't know if you lay awake in the small hours justifying your decision to yourself.*

*My own thoughts have taken me to a more rational understanding that, for the majority, the necessity of making such a decision will happen only once in your life, if at all.*

*If you choose to absolve yourself of all responsibility, by text message, to the woman you ostensibly loved and the child you had said you wanted, on the basis that you have the biological capability of doing so, you cannot claim that this is not representative. Sometimes, we must be judged by our one-offs.*

*Having consulted my own male friends, many of whom are fathers themselves, I take some level of comfort in knowing that they are all outraged at your behaviour. Conflicted obviously, by the thought that, in a sea of wonderful, kind and feeling men, I've somehow and unluckily found the anomaly.*

*Which leads me to my next question: what do your own friends think? Your own best friend, a step father to two small girls, and whose wife was left, like me, by the father of her children. I cannot begin to believe that he would have kept quiet, having been so close to the destruction that an absent father leaves.*

*In my head, I will his wife to tell you of the devastation of seeing a young child cry that their father rejected them. I want her to shake you violently and tell you truthfully of the poverty and the depression and the loneliness of raising a child alone.*

*I think of you often; almost every hour your sweet face swims to the fore of my mind and floors me. What are you doing and who are you with? I wonder if you're with another woman now, someone who will no doubt know nothing of me and your baby.*

*Are your rolling over in bed, sleepily snuggling close to her whilst, down the road, I lie awake, alone, with our baby kicking so furiously into my soft belly. Will she laugh like I did at your idiosyncrasies, those peculiar bedtime routines you so rigidly adhered to. Hands, face, teeth. Vest off. Earplugs in as the clock turned eleven. Phone set to flight mode. Kiss on the cheek. Sleep.*

*I want to call you every day. I want you to know and to understand the reality of life for me now you're gone. The knowing glances from the midwives, now that you've forcibly put me into that stigmatised bracket, the hated demographic of the single mother. Those boxes on the forms I never thought I'd have to tick.*

*I know you will never receive the bitter, biting comments that I do, the blunt inference of promiscuity and irresponsibility. Though I know it's not your fault, that it's indicative of society's ingrained perceptions of women and sexuality, I wonder, if the tables were turned, if I walked away from my baby after birth to leave you picking up the pieces of my selfishness and flagrant disregard for others, a mewling baby in tow, would you be treated the same?*

*Would your aunties raise their unkind eyebrows at your irresponsibility? Would your friends mutter slyly to each other that perhaps you should have used a condom? I suspect people would praise you as a hero, a magnanimous human being who took on the responsibility of parenting alone without complaint.*

*Most of all, though, I think about the impact of your choice on the life of our baby. I worry endlessly about the space you will leave behind, what your absence will create in this child and what it will take away.*

*The thought of our son or daughter, aged five, asking where daddy is and why doesn't he come to watch the swimming gala, haunts me daily. That when I think of how her history, her sense of belonging and her identity will only ever be half sketched I'm filled with a level of rage towards you that I never thought possible in meek, mild me*

*The wonderful, human parts of you, your patient, gentle kindness like the time you spent two frustrating hours trying attempting to explain the rules of cricket so I could share in your life, our child will never have the benefit of.*

*Will my parenting, my character, and the fierce love I already feel for this child, ever compensate for the bits they wont be able to take from the beautiful parts of you?*

*I want you to know that your absence is felt. That I will do this because I have to. But it hurts. Dina*

*It's been almost 7 months since the last time you saw your child, and that's only because his Great Grandmother emailed me. It's been over a year since you've contacted him yourself. There are no birthday phone calls. No parent teacher conferences, or meetings with the adjustment counselor. No foot ball practices, or games. No doctors appointments, student of the month celebrations, late night emergency room visits, no fishing trips.*

*You're not here to see your child tear himself to pieces because he has to come to the terms that you left him without an explanation. You're not here to convince him that he is worthy of love, and that he matters. And just when I think he's starting to heal, the bandaid gets ripped off, and we have to start the process all over.*

*I am thankful. I am thankful for my husband. Who day after day loves a little boy that he never had to. That no matter how hard my son pushes him away, he never stops trying for him to show him he is wanted. I am thankful he HAS a dad who is worthy of that title, even if it isnt his biological one.*

*I am thankful for MY father, who makes sure to include him in EVERYTHING you never did. He teaches my son about hard work, and doing things for people not because you get paid to do them, but because you love the people you are helping. Hes being taught to be compassionate, that if you have the ability to help, you should. About obligation, and responsibility, and leadership, and love, and how ALL those things intertwine.*

*I am thankful for my male friends, who include him, and consider him, and treat him like he belongs. Who take him under his wing and acknowledge him, and bond with him - making strides in efforts you always deemed beneath you. These men, with their own families, and their own jobs, and their own obligations have set aside more time to dedicate to investing in your child than you have.*

*People that do not HAVE to love my son, love him, and they love him HARD. Because we need him to know that even though you are incapable of doing it, that he is worth it. That he deserves it.*

*I suppose, I have to come to peace with the idea that you will never get it together for him.*

*I will have to come to peace with the fact that despite that we BOTH know the truth, you will parade me around like "a monster who wont LET you see your son" and your friends will believe that. The most dangerous lie we can tell ourselves is the one we begin to believe.*

*I have to come to peace knowing that you will NEVER mend the wounds you created in this wonderful, innocent boy. And have left cleaning up the pieces to me, and his step father.*

*I may have to forgive you for what you have done to him, because that is the ONLY way I can help him heal.*

*But I will NEVER forget what you've done. I will never forget the nights I've held my son while he's cried himself to sleep. Or the outbursts we've settled when hes waited for HOURS for you to pick him up, and never show up. Or the breakdown he has every time his phone calls get forwarded to voicemail. I will NEVER forget the way you've made my child feel, but I need to focus on healing him from the damage you have caused, so I need to forgive you.*

*I wish you the best in your endeavors.*

*Even calling you my "father" brings about intense pains, countless memories of tossing in my bed wondering why I wasn't enough for you, and tears to last a lifetime. While I am wondering whether or not to allow you into my life, the question tosses in my mind: Why wasn't I enough for you and how could you abandon me?*

*I've spent years trying to come up with a logical reason as to why you haven't made an appearance in my life, and nothing seems to ring a bell. I needed you to help me grow up. I needed not only my mother's guidance but the guidance of a father. I needed a man to tell me that the boy I liked was no good for me. I needed that father-daughter protection when the first boy I loved broke my heart. I needed a man as a defender.*

*It sickens me that one can go to bed at night, carry on with their life, knowing their own blood-line is suffering from sadness and abandonment. It boggles my mind that you can maintain strong relationships with your other children, but me? No, I wasn't good enough for you. I wasn't what you wanted and that's fine. But give me some explanations as to what I did wrong. What made me so different from the rest?*

*Due to the horrible choices you've made, I've learned to live a life without two parents like every child should. It's clear to me that you don't have a heart; don't care about anyone other than yourself. You shouldn't think randomly attempting to be in my life after my 19 years on this Earth that I would be willing to let you in with open arms. You should be begging for my forgiveness, begging to get to know someone as strong as I am.*

*I just want to say thank you. Thank you for showing me the kind of person NOT to be. Thank you for making me the strongest person I could ever be. And I feel sorry for you. I'm sorry you don't get to know someone as independent, caring, strong and successful as me. But that wasn't my choice, it was yours. And I'm glad you chose to go your own way because I've managed to be the best person I could be without your help, which probably wouldn't even be useful.*

*Sorry you couldn't see your own blood grow up; you could but you chose not to.*

*With extreme hatred,*

*Your "daughter."*

www.ingramcontent.com/pod-product-compliance
Lightning Source LLC
Chambersburg PA
CBHW070543170426
43200CB00011B/2527